MW01042327

"Diversity, like gravity, is all around us and is therefore beyond dispute or debate; the challenge of leveraging that diversity—the work of inclusion—remains, however, unfinished and unfulfilled. Joe Watson offers a practical, highly readable, and compelling case for inclusion and one that should reenergize those who suffer from 'diversity fatigue.'"

> —Gilbert F. Casellas, former Chairman, Equal Employment Opportunity Commission and Of Counsel, Mintz Levin Cohn Ferris Glovsky and Popeo, PC

"Going forward, an organization's success will largely depend on is ability to identify, attract, and retain top talent from a shrinking and increasingly diverse talent pool. *Without Excuses* offers useful, straightforward guidance aimed at helping organizations win in an increasingly competitive marketplace."

> —W. H. Easter III, Chairman, CEO, and President, Duke Energy Field Services

"Joe Watson approaches the issue of diversity through the simple lens of things that either 'can' or 'can't' be done. He argues convincingly that the liberal use of the word 'can't' reflects the distortion that the issues of diversity and race have injected into the normal course of business. *Without Excuses* offers the reader an opportunity to regain their 'business' footing on the issue of diversity and return to the traditional path of business—where strategies are developed, plans executed, and the successful rewarded."

> —Stacey J. Mobley, Senior Vice President, Chief Administrative Officer, and General Counsel, DuPont

"This book is 'must read' for every HR professional and every executive and manager who claims to believe in fairness, justice, inclusiveness, and profitability. It not only identifies problems and excuses in addressing diversity, especially racial diversity, but it also provides simple and effective solutions. If you trust it and follow it, you will benefit from it both individually and organizationally."

—John E. Jacob, Executive Vice President and Chief Communications Officer, Anheuser-Busch Companies, Inc., and former President and CEO, National Urban League

WITHOUT EXCUSES

UNLEASH THE **POWER**
OF **DIVERSITY** TO
BUILD YOUR BUSINESS

Joe Watson

St. Martin's Press ⋙ New York

www.stmartins.com

Book design by Richard Oriolo

LIBRARY OF CONGRESS CATALOGING-IN-
PUBLICATION DATA

Watson, Joe, 1966–
    Without excuses : unleash the power of
    diversity to build your business / Joe
    Watson.—1st ed.
        p. cm.
    Includes bibliographical references.
    ISBN-13: 978-0-312-36160-0
    ISBN-10: 0-312-36160-2
    1. Minority professional employees—
Recruiting—United States. 2. Diversity in
the workplace—United States. I. Title.

HF5549.5.R44W38 2006
658.3008—dc22   2006047467

First Edition: November 2006

10 9 8 7 6 5 4 3 2 1

CONTENTS

ACKNOWLEDGMENTS

To say that I have learned a lot and been humbled by this writing effort would be an incredible understatement. Through it all I have been driven by a passion to bring the "truth" forward and I have been supported by many wonderful people who have played a significant role in the development of this book and Joe Watson. I would like to thank several of them here.

Placing the "we find diverse talent" stake in the ground required an incredible commitment and team. Mark Sucoloski and Stephen Johnson were true early partners in this effort and contributed much to the philosophy and tactics found throughout this book.

In many cases, one of the greatest challenges of any writer is finding a "partner in thought" who truly shares your "voice" and, at times, embodies your spirit—my sincere thanks to Mary Porter for her tremendous contribution in helping to capture the spirit of *Without Excuses*.

Our current Without Excuses family led by Gene Venuto and Deb Cullerton has been an incredible source of support and guidance throughout this effort. It is a great relief to know that all is well while I'm off "creating."

Throughout my career there have been key individuals and groups who have provided critical guidance and assisted me in making more of life's "right" decisions: Willie King, Governor Mark R. Warner, Barry Johnson, Nicholas Perrins, Carl Brooks,

David Dreyer, Sid Smith, Tracy White, Reggie Brown, Maurice Jones, The Exchange Network, Chuck Mills, Catherine Murphy, Mario Morino, Belle Wheelan, Bob Greene, Dick Clouser, Greg and Lisa Giles, Michael Warren, and Mike Clarke.

I would like to thank Joshua Simons for his constant vigilance in capturing the essence of *Without Excuses*. Alas, none of this energy and goodwill goes anywhere without a skilled guide who can help one navigate the maze that is publishing—my agent, Peter Miller, is hands down one of New York's best.

My editor at St. Martin's Press, Phil Revzin, has been incredibly supportive—from being our internal champion to demonstrating the patience of a saint when answering one of my many questions. My sincere thanks also to editorial assistant Lauren Hodge, who handled my almost daily queries and challenges with tremendous grace and aplomb.

When one thinks about all the reasons why this effort was successful, it really starts and ends with a terrific family. I am fortunate to have a wonderful wife, Leann, who has been my partner in this life's journey. It is through her grace that I am available to help so many. I would also like to thank my children, Mia, Morgan, and Sydney, for they are my true inspiration to create a world where the king of excuses, "We can't find any . . ." is extinct. To my parents, Nat and Marie, for setting the example throughout my life that the pursuit of life's path with excellence and compassion is simply the only way, and to my siblings, Natlie, Nicole, and Michael, for their never-ending support.

Finally, to all the talented people of color and women who strive every day to achieve their goals—"Thank you." Our daily interactions have emboldened me to create a world free of "Excuses" and challenge others to do the same.

FOREWORD

Without Excuses is without exception a breath of fresh air, a comprehensive and refreshing look at Corporate America's relationship with diversity over the decades and a road map to help companies gain serious traction in making the business case for diversity. In author Joe Watson's mind, the business case for diversity is simply about implementing solid business strategy—or more important, succeeding in today's business climate by meeting current demands and preparing for the future by rising to the challenges and opportunities offered by the diverse marketplace.

With more than 100 million people of color in the United States, Joe knows that Corporate America's global competitiveness depends on reinvention. Companies must enhance their capabilities to capture diverse markets and hire diverse business talent capable of effectively responding to the needs of this growing consumer base. Supported by labor and market statistics, he shows how this capability will depend on corporate creativity, flexibility, and leadership that enables companies to move outside of old paradigms and comfort zones to gain a competitive edge. *Without Excuses* exudes an inspirational tone focusing on what *we* can do in Corporate America to make it a more welcoming and productive enterprise for all of us.

Contrasting companies that continued to make hackneyed excuses such as "we can't find any diverse candidates" or "diverse professionals don't want to work here" with innovators like Pitney Bowes who "began a proven documented commitment to diversity in the 1940s," Joe draws on his vast knowledge and experience as a corporate diversity recruiter and business leader to define the landscape, present enlightened options, and highlight examples of companies successfully using diversity to build their businesses.

In Joe's assessment, a company's acceptance of its inability to make the business case for diversity is not as much about racism or ill will as about fear. The subtitle to this gem of a book announces that there is a better option: Unleash the Power of Diversity to Build Your Business. Joe is right on point, outlining straightforward, easy to understand, benchmarking strategies that show you how.

In chapters as clear and focused as his advice and writing style, Joe helps corporations not only 'fess up to their ineffective business practices and beliefs but shows them how to also strip away excuses robbing them of business. After laying this foundation, this workbook, written in a conversational tone, provides guidelines to help you get to work on corporate reinvention—setting priorities, preparing a company's internal climate for change, refining internal and external messages, building multicultural networks, recruiting and retaining diverse talent, and most important, setting benchmarks and assessment protocols to measure success.

Supporting his strategies is a wealth of data: bibliographies, lists of professional organizations and top companies for diversity, as well as higher-education institutions serving minority populations, and Web sites supporting diversity recruitment and other business needs.

Without Excuses is a much needed business resource that will inform CEOs and serve the needs of business executives, senior human resources leaders, chief diversity officers, and other executives with responsibilities for effectively managing the diverse workplace.

Joe provides a fresh voice and insights to old questions about why leaders fail to deal with diversity in Corporate America. *Without Excuses* addresses the subject of diversity and race in an open, unapologetic manner that elevates race to a positive four-letter word that compels senior leaders to see engaging race as a business opportunity rather than a burden, as a business strategy rather than a social mandate.

This is a must-read, a valuable learning tool, and executive road map to make the journey of traveling this business course as important as each company's expected destination.

Carl Brooks
President and CEO
The Executive Leadership Council

INTRODUCTION

I s bigotry more powerful than greed? This question hit me like a ton of bricks when I first focused my practice on diversity recruiting. Previously, I had been an executive recruiter working largely with majority professionals, and the world of recruiting had seemed fairly methodical and efficient—like most business processes. But now, as I began to discuss ways to build a diverse workforce with clients, associates, and candidates, I was taken aback by the resounding chorus of negativity coming from all sides. Clients pushed back, saying, "We can't find any minorities" or "They don't want to move here." Associates pushed back, saying, "No one really cares about this stuff. It's all just lip service to avoid getting sued or have people picketing in front of their offices." And candidates pushed back, saying, "I don't want to be identified as a minority. In fact, I've removed all references to being a person of color from my résumé." (How tremendously sad to deny one's fundamental identity!) These comments, while they may sound extreme, are accurate representations of the mood of each group, and run directly counter to one of the most valued elements of business—a focus on results!

The lessons in this book are critical to the success of your enterprise. The lurking threat for everyone is competition. Which establishment will be recognized as the employer of choice, the provider of choice, the educational institution of choice, depends on who can lead with a successful strategic plan for ten, twenty, even fifty years down the road. I promise everyone reading this book: Your competitors are working hard to position themselves for the future. They may even get the whole idea of a "diversity dividend" and be working on a diversity strategy. But the good news for you is that most will fail. They will say they are committed, but they won't be. They will fail because they'll be using the same old excuses to stay in their comfort zone. A comfort zone is a powerful thing—and it can cripple your business.

I am a person driven by challenge and inspired by the opportunity to alter perceptions—so the sensitive climate around this otherwise very practical process of recruiting diverse professionals moved me to action. As a recruiter, as an African-American, and most of all, as a logical businessman, I needed to

understand: How could this reluctant attitude toward multiculturalism in the workplace *still* be so prevalent today? Especially
when the business case for building a diverse workforce has
been so undeniably and forcefully articulated?

According to the 2000 census report, there are now more
than 100 million people of color living in the United States. If
your company makes things, sells things, or services things, this
number has enormous implications. These people of color are
your customers. They are your suppliers. They are your workforce. To ignore them is to stick your head in the sand on a critical and growing competitive issue—even to neglect your
fiduciary duty.

I know—many of you reading this are thinking, "Well,
that's not us. We have a diversity plan. We are doing enough."
But based on my extensive experience working with corporate
America—and the hard, cold facts of ongoing workplace
disparities—I am going to challenge you on that. You may have
words on paper, you may have that hint of goodwill in the air,
but you probably are not doing enough.

In fact, companies throughout America are still very
much struggling with diversity. And it is my observation that
they have allowed a mind-numbing list of excuses to enable,
even validate, their lack of progress. The king of all excuses:
"We can't find any diverse candidates." Not only is this
patently false—as I will discuss in greater detail later in this
book—but it contradicts long-standing, deeply ingrained business standards of practice. Since when did it become okay to
say, "I can't?" To my knowledge, in the competitive world of
business, senior leaders who "can't" get things done "can't"
have their jobs anymore. Yet somehow, with respect to diversity, "I tried, I tried really, really hard, but I just can't" has

come to be accepted as a valid excuse for failing to achieve an important strategic goal.

The more I talked to these companies, the more I began to wonder, Why are they so ineffective and so willing to fail when it comes to diversity? What could make otherwise logical and efficient corporations so illogical and inefficient on this one point? Could it be—was it possible—that deeply ingrained bigotry had proven to be more powerful than the desire to compete in the marketplace?

As I've gone about my work of helping companies attract, recruit, and retain diverse professionals, I've researched this question. I've facilitated countless working groups and spoken formally and informally to dozens of executives struggling with workplace diversity. I have been privy to some of the darkest secrets that an organization can have. I have spoken with many candidates of color either exiting companies or operating from within, and I have become well versed in their struggles around acceptance, access, and succession. Through all of this, I believe I have arrived at an answer—and thankfully, it is a positive one. By and large, corporate America is not racist. Corporate executives are not hiding some deep-down desire to discriminate and segregate. No—I've come to the conclusion that corporate America is just . . . afraid.

Most of us don't understand cultures that are different from our own, and we are scared to try. This may sound like a pretty basic problem, one that is easy to solve, but trust me, it is no small thing. The fear surrounding racial issues in the workplace has caused the equivalent of a coast-to-coast blackout. It has rendered otherwise competent people completely incapable of normal business practices. I refer to this condition as "the suspension of business logic." In this condition, fear and ignorance have the power to turn even the most polished, intelligent, and articulate person into a babbling drone prone to totally ineffectual conduct.

We in corporate America are so paralyzed by racial issues that we often can't even talk about the most basic things. For example, we don't even know how—or whether—to refer to someone's race anymore. We might say, "Bill is bla—Afro-Amer—I mean Afri-Amer, I mean colored," and then, "Oops, did I say that out loud?" Obviously, I'm kidding here—but you get my drift. Even though race is one of the first things we notice about a person, we don't have the first clue how to address it for fear we might offend someone, look stupid, or get sued.

I know this may sound simplistic, but I truly believe this awkwardness, this discomfort, this unwillingness to venture beyond our own comfort zone, is at the root of the diversity paralysis affecting organizations throughout America today. It is this awkwardness that interferes with the otherwise natural process of hiring and promoting diverse professionals. It keeps introductions and conversations from happening naturally; it keeps majority and minority business networks separate and apart. And it is this problem of disconnected networks that is the biggest reason why companies fail to make progress in diversity recruiting.

Additionally, despite the challenges that this level of discomfort and awkwardness can generate in a work environment, many companies have pushed forward with their diversity efforts and now find themselves in a different place: the land of "diversity fatigue." The reality is that pushing this boulder of change uphill can be a truly draining experience for all involved. Employees must be thinking, "Here we go again! Someone has decided we should start our 'New Diversity Initiative' for the third or fourth time." And for the internal diversity advocates, all of the starts and stops, resistance, and emotional upheaval associated with affecting change exact a heavy toll on body, spirit, and mind. All this is due to the intractability caused by the suspension of business logic.

One particular experience I had readily demonstrates the impact of this suspended state. Executives at one of my client companies had been struggling for years to build a diverse workforce. They were, like most, very good people who were bright, capable, and committed to the success of their enterprise. Their business would be considered highly attractive by most outsiders. As a result, they had little difficulty attracting the best employees to the organization. Most of their hires came through their referral network, due to their status within their industry and the loyalty of their employees. Since most of their employees were white, the resultant new hires were white as well. To their great credit, they recognized that in order to change the "complexion" of their workforce they would have to do things differently.

We decided to target several positions in an area that offered great promise for attracting a diverse pool of candidates. The clients readily admitted that they were aware of *no* viable candidates of color within their industry. In our role, we brought forward several viable candidates of color, in short order. Clearly, they were surprised—the good kind of surprised— that these people were available. Quickly, we decided to move the candidates through the company's interview process.

One candidate's interactions with the company illustrate the challenges that the suspension of business logic poses to any effort to diversify. The candidate was extremely strong and had actually performed the job function sought both as an individual contributor and as a manager. After a successful day of

interviews, I connected with the client for a review. The feedback was generally positive, but there was a concern that made
his further progress unlikely. He was deemed to be "too arrogant" or "too full of himself." The evidence for this conclusion:
the candidate had brought to the interview a binder containing
letters of appreciation from prior managers and customers,
copies of certificates of achievement, and newspaper clippings.
The hiring managers viewed this binder as a "bragging book"
and therefore incompatible with their culture of subtle success.
Some of you reading this may be thinking, "Well, Joe, that
doesn't seem all that unreasonable."

I can appreciate that sentiment, but let's look at it this way.
The candidate knew he was going to interview with one of the
industry leaders. He also knew that he had accomplished quite
a bit in a relatively short business career. Given that he was a
person of color, he also believed that as he was recounting his
experiences in the interviews there would likely be those who
doubted that he had actually achieved all the things that he
shared. Therefore, he presented the binder simply to provide
tangible proof of his achievements. As I shared this view with
the hiring managers, they acknowledged that this thought process had never entered their mind, and it led to a deeper discussion about their unwritten expectations of candidates and how
those expectations must change if they were to successfully har-
ness the full potential of the workforce.

Now ask yourself, What must it be like to walk into interviews expecting that the words you are speaking will *not* be believed, and to need to present physical evidence of your
achievements? In a business that operates free of the awkwardness and discomfort that diversity introduces, an interview process can be refined to allow the interaction of people to happen

naturally and for deliberations around capabilities and qualifications to be performed in a fair and uniform way.

Fortunately, these are all problems with solutions. For years now I have been helping organizations large and small move past their issues with diversity and achieve real results. I've worked with in-house recruiters, human resources professionals, and executives across industries to push through the excuses and fears crippling their diversity initiatives. I've helped them to refocus on their diversity goals, and develop sound business strategies for achieving them. And I've helped them to apply the principles in this book to locate and recruit the very best diversity talent. These companies got results. If you follow the steps I've outlined in this book, you will get results too.

This book focuses primarily on racial diversity, but its principles and techniques can be applied to any kind of diversity—gender, age, cultural, religious. It is divided into two parts: "Get Real and Get Ready" and "Connect and Build."

In the first part, I will challenge you to get past your issues with diversity and focus on your true objectives. Specifically, I will help you to:

- strip away the excuses and myths blocking your path to success;
- outline your organization's business case for diversity;
- clarify your priorities;
- straighten out your diversity recruiting practices; and
- critically assess your internal and external messaging about diversity.

Once you've "gotten real" about your diversity initiative and put your house in order, you will be ready to build lasting diversity by recruiting and hiring talented multicultural professionals. In the second part of this book I will challenge you to:

- move past your comfort zone to connect with new and different networks of diverse professionals;
- use a variety of proven techniques to identify talented diverse professionals;
- commit the time and resources required to "build a bench" of diverse talent; and
- establish effective new strategies for measuring success and ensuring accountability.

At the end of each chapter (and within some chapters) you will find an "Action Plan." The Action Plan is a series of direct questions that will drive you toward a clearer understanding of where your organization truly is relative to your diversity effort. The questions are written in such a way that the truth is the only acceptable outcome. I strongly urge you to view your answers as an opportunity to look into your personal and organizational "mirror." The mirror provides an opportunity to remove the corporate/societal rhetoric and pressures and simply deal with your environment as it is. I cannot emphasize strongly enough that you cannot make true, meaningful, sustainable progress with regard to diversity until you are willing to answer these questions directly. This book can be used cover to cover from the senior-executive to administrative levels of your organization. It is a great tool to facilitate discussions surrounding diversity among team members and provides a universal foundation upon which expectations can be built. Finally, it serves as an essential guide, full of resources and techniques, to help any member of your staff who is responsible for recruiting diverse talent into your organization.

The book closes with a set of appendices that I lightheartedly call the "Here We Are Collection." All too often, I have heard from many quarters, "We can't find any . . . ," so I decided that I would tell everyone where we are, in case anyone wants to come looking for us after reading this book. You will find great information on building diversity, diversity recruiting Web sites, diverse organizations and clubs, media options, multicultural colleges and universities, and much more. All of these tools are focused on eliminating the excuses and driving the expected results.

So where will your company be by the end of the twenty-first century? Will you have exploded with growth by dominating emerging multicultural markets? Will you have crushed the competition by hiring the brightest and most innovative talent, regardless of race? Or will you be standing still while your competitors pass you by? If you are still stuck—well, you can't say you didn't see it coming or that you didn't know what to do. Those excuses will be gone. After reading this book, you'll have a clear idea of where your company currently stands on diversity, and you'll be able to form a plan so you can move forward confidently, knowing without a doubt that you can find the best diverse talent, *without excuses.*

HOW TO USE
THIS BOOK

A re you really ready to change? Or are you searching for information to maintain and support the status quo?

If you've picked up this book, you are likely ready for answers to the vexing questions that a diversity effort can raise across your enterprise. The good news is that this book will answer many of those vexing questions. However, this book is like any other toolkit—you must follow the instructions to produce a quality product. I feel strongly that it isn't enough simply to put this information out there. I want you to use this material to achieve maximum impact. Also, I am removing one more set of excuses before you go any further. You know, the "it doesn't really apply to me," "this is written for the rank and file," "this must be for the executives" types of excuses. As you will discover, this book has a learning path for everyone, and therefore it can become a key part of the diversity foundation throughout your organization, at all levels.

Each chapter opens with an overview of the critical topic area, followed by a series of observations, examples, and insights focused on helping you assess where your organization truly is relative to each element of the diversity continuum. Additionally, I focus on helping you identify the likely stumbling blocks and further enhance the potential of your organization to move toward your ideal state as quickly as possible. I conclude each chapter with an Action Plan that will allow you to gather concrete data and develop firm plans which will ensure your progress.

I hope that you will read this book from cover to cover. However, I also want each leadership group within the enterprise to have a specific understanding of what this book offers it—thus the guidance outlined in the next several pages. Again, no excuses here: whether you have the time to read the entire book or just some, the time you spend reading will be most beneficial to you and your organization's diversity effort.

Here's where to begin: take a look at Figure 1.1 (p. 14), which illustrates how organizations create and roll out a business strategy. As you will see throughout this book, companies that are serious about diversity treat diversification as a business strategy critical to their success, and not a nice-to-have initiative. Typically, critical strategies are developed and released by the organization's leadership to the functions responsible for designing and running the implementation plan. At this level, execution usually has two pathways: the group directly responsible for leading and designing the implementation (the direct contributors) and those parts of the organization that have an influence on the success of the strategy (the indirect contributors). Diversity strategies should not be treated any differently.

Use Figure 1.1 as a "diversity directory" to determine your role in this strategy. Locate that role in this chapter and follow the recommended steps on using the book to implement true change. These steps articulate a basic process that will help you develop a strategy while weaving in the information and recommendations from the book.

ROLE:
EXECUTIVE LEADERSHIP

In large companies, leadership comes from the board of directors, C-level executives, and other senior executive team members. In medium and small companies, leadership may be driven down further into the director and senior manager level. Another way to make this assessment: Where are the decisions made and the strategies developed that direct and grow the company? The answer indicates your leadership chain. It is critical for this group to determine the direction, provide the support, and hold everyone accountable for a successful outcome. Therefore:

Figure 1.1

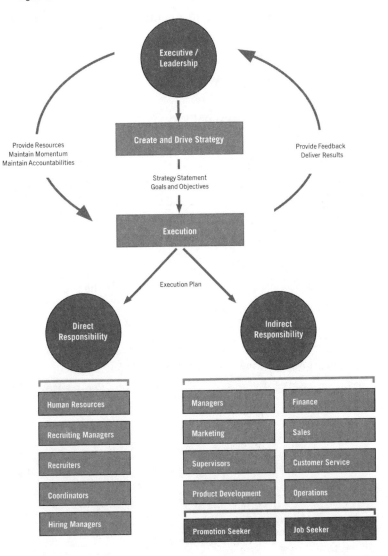

Step 1: Preparing the Strategy

- Read chapter 1 and look for the excuses that may pervade your organization and stifle your strategy yet again. Be prepared to combat these excuses using the logic and experiences outlined.
- Read chapter 2 and arm yourself with the facts and figures that provide the fuel for change.

Step 2: Unifying the Vision

- Ask the executive leadership team to read chapters 1 and 2 and complete the get-real audit in the Action Plan at the end of chapter 1.
- Conduct a facilitated discussion to surface the beliefs and understand the excuses that exist or have been used in the organization. Be frank and honest while being mindful of groupthink and other behaviors that allow beliefs to drift back to status quo.
- When you achieve true recognition and buy-in from the leadership team, move on to building your individualized business case for diversity. Develop this through facilitated discussions guided by the Action Plan at the end of chapter 2.

Step 3: Outlining the Strategy and Goals and Creating Standards and Accountability

- Convene the entire leadership team to craft a specific strategy relevant to your organization. This "strategy statement" articulates your position and expectations, and it is the vehicle by which your decisions are communicated to the people responsible for implementing the strategy. It is important for the results of this plan to be linked to other priorities and long-term objectives. The Action Plan at the end of chapter 3 will help you establish some of the specific components of your diversity strategy.

- Go to chapter 9 and its Action Plan and select an appropriate series of metrics to set the expectations of your staff when communicating to your staff and the people who will be executing the strategy. People are frequently tempted to wait until implementation to think about measurements, and they rarely consider accountability when it comes to this topic. What an organization elects to measure (e.g., market share, stock price, employee growth) speaks loudly to its employees about what's really important.

Step 4: Incorporating the Strategy into the Business

- It is essential for the standards and measures of success created in step 3 to be incorporated into the organization's goals and objectives process. Meet with human resources and direct this incorporation.
- To ensure accountability from the senior level to the operational level, leadership should also require the standards to be integrated into the existing performance management process.
- Now after a quarterly review, leadership will have data points required to monitor progress and make adjustments to the strategy or its execution well in advance of a potential failure.

ROLE:
LEADERSHIP—DIRECT EXECUTION

As the name implies, people with these roles (people in human resources and diversity leaders) are directly responsible for translating the leadership team's strategy into the tactics and initiatives that generate results. You become the arms, eyes, and ears of the leadership team, and your feedback will be critical to gauging success and prompting adjustments.

Step 1: Preparing and Receiving the Handoff

- Read chapters 1–3 to frame appropriately the strategy crafted by the leadership team.
- Request a strategy statement from leadership, and the facts and figures that support its business case for diversity.

Step 2: Spreading the Word, Communicating the Standards

- Read chapter 4.
- Inform leadership of any glaring discrimination issues that have to be addressed before implementing the strategy.
- Meet with line managers and supervisors. Share the strategy statement, and facilitate a discussion around the business case. Use the get-real audit from chapter 1's Action Plan to surface beliefs and excuses that might prevent the management team's true buy-in.
- Demonstrate how the strategy has been incorporated into the goals and objectives and how everyone will be held

accountable through the performance management process.

Step 3: Formulating the Execution Plan

- Read chapters 5–8 and formulate an execution plan to make the strategy come to life. Pay specific attention to the messages in these chapters as they relate to:
  - attraction
  - recruitment
  - retention
  - networking
  - messaging

Step 4: Assessing Resources and Rolling Out

- Review the completed execution plan with leadership.
- Assure that the plan aligns with the organization's vision and strategy.
- Request the resources needed to execute the plan. If the plan aligns with the strategy, but the resources are not available and do not become available, your strategy is dead.
- Once approvals and resources are in place, roll out the execution plan complete with accountabilities to the people responsible for the day-to-day actions.

ROLE:
DAY-TO-DAY DIRECT EXECUTION

Recruiters, coordinators, staffing managers, people working with outside agencies, and hiring managers will be responsible for completing the activities that move the strategy from words on a page to a business reality. So it is essential that you be comfortable and fully skilled in areas that may be foreign to your standard operating procedures. This process will ask you to stretch your comfort zone and your networks, and increase the organization's outreach and the depth of its "bench."

Step 1: Preparing and Receiving the Handoff

- Read chapters 1–3 to frame appropriately the strategy crafted by the leadership team.
- Conduct the get-real audit in the Action Plan at the end of chapter 1.
- Request a copy of the execution plan that pertains to your function.
- Examine the goals and objectives you will be responsible for maintaining, and look at how they fit into your performance review. Discuss with your supervisor any areas of concern you have.

Step 2: Learning and Adjusting Your Process

- Read chapters 6, 7, and 8.
- Follow the Action Plans at the end of each chapter to fill in any gaps in your process.

- Incorporate the learning and suggestions that broaden your reach and change the way you work with diverse candidates into daily routines and workflows.
- Monitor your actions to see if you are on course to hit your targets.
- Provide regular feedback so that any gaps in the execution plan are addressed early in the process.

ROLE: INDIRECT INVOLVEMENT WITH THE EXECUTION PLAN

If you find yourself in this category, chances are you were handed this book and did not pick it up on your own. Or you have a vested interest in the outcome of the process and you are forward-thinking enough to recognize that which many of your colleagues have overlooked. Your biggest contribution here is in your ability to reach out on behalf of the organization into new professional and social circles. Your work product must also be in direct alignment with the diversity strategy. You will see examples in the book where a misalignment from product development or marketing caused serious harm to the strategy and to the entire organization. So resist any temptation to push this aside and leave it up to the people in human resources. This affects everyone, and everyone has a role in the strategy's success.

Step 1: Preparing and Receiving the Handoff

- Read chapters 1–3 to frame appropriately the strategy crafted by the leadership team.

- Conduct the get-real audit in the Action Plan at the end of chapter 1.
- Request a copy of the execution plan and the goals and objectives that pertain to your function.
- Examine the benchmarks and standards you will be responsible for maintaining, and look at how they fit into your performance review. Discuss with your supervisor any areas of concern you have.

Step 2: Representing the Message

- Read chapter 5.
- List the areas where you affect the internal and external messaging of the organization. How can you bring messaging in alignment with the strategy and the goals and objectives?

Step 3: Building Networks

- Read chapter 6.
- Formulate your networking plan by completing the Action Plan at the end of the chapter. This plan is directed toward recruiters, but the steps can be generalized to anyone who can help the organization broaden its reach through networking.

ROLE:
JOB OR PROMOTION SEEKER

As a job seeker or promotion seeker you've shown insight by picking up this book. This book isn't a typical career-management book or interviewing-technique guide. Instead, you will gain deeper insight into the thought process of hiring executives and their needs and concerns about diversity. You will also see how leading organizations that truly value diversity provide the resources, focus, and accountabilities needed to succeed. So for the job seeker, *Without Excuses* guides you through a thorough evaluation process that can be utilized to assess potential employers. It also outlines a way to leverage your own contributions to any diversity strategy during the hiring or promotion process.

Step 1: Understanding the Environment

- Read chapter 1 and the accompanying get-real audit in the Action Plan. This process will sensitize you to the excuses commonly cited by organizations to explain why they are not more diverse. You will be able to recognize these before or as they emerge in your evaluation process.

Step 2: Evaluating the Organization

- Read chapter 4 and use all your resources (e.g., networks, search engines) to assure that the organization has its house in order and that there are no glaring discrimination issues. If you are just beginning a search, couple this with a review of appendix C, "Top Companies for Diversity." These organizations have set demanding but achievable diversity benchmarks and standards.
- Read chapter 5 and further sensitize yourself to internal and external messaging. These subtle but prophetic clues

demonstrate how serious an organization is about competing in a multicultural world.

- Look for published diversity statements, which are often
  found on companies' Web sites or in their annual reports.
  Does your evaluation match these printed intentions?

Step 3: Assessing Your Potential Contribution to the Organization

- Read chapters 2 and 3 to learn all of the possible ways successful diversity strategies can impact the bottom line of an
  organization.
- Use the organization's published diversity strategy and
  identify any initiatives and goals to which you can make a
  contribution. Link your contribution to a specific business
  case outcome and be prepared to articulate the effect you
  can have on the organization.
- Read chapters 6 through 8 to gain an insider's perspective
  on the talent-acquisition process. Which part of your network would benefit the organization's diversity strategy?
- Create a personal contribution inventory, a document that
  lists all of the diversity assets you bring to the table. You
  should reference each of the appendices and use these
  topics as thought starters for your inventory. For example,
  in which diverse professional or student groups are you
  active? What ties do you have to historically diverse colleges and universities? Which diverse publications do you
  read?
- Look for opportunities to offer appropriate examples from
  your contribution inventory during career-advancement

conversations. These can be formal job interviews, or informal discussions with colleagues and superiors.

- In chapter 8, you will learn how companies segment and stay connected to their top talent. Use the insights from this chapter to become proactive and partner with recruiters so you are kept informed when new opportunities arise.

Now that you have identified your path, let's move quickly into the core of *Without Excuses*.

PART I

GET REAL AND GET READY

1

STRIP AWAY
THE EXCUSES

To succeed at diversity recruiting, you must strip away your disabling excuses and get real. Getting real means you no longer tolerate the use of the word "can't." It means you start to recognize suspended business logic when you see it, and treat diversity like every other important strategic initiative.

With respect to diversity, it is my experience that organizations typically fall into one of four categories: obstructionist (they do as little as possible), defensive (they do only that which is legally or politically expedient), accommodative (they meet legal and ethical requirements, and perhaps a bit more), or proactive (they act before they have to). Do any of these sound familiar? If your organization falls into one of the first three categories, this chapter was written especially for you. It is time for you to look in the mirror and tell the truth. Pitney Bowes looked into the mirror and began a proven, documented commitment to diversity in the 1940s. One aspect of its mission statement declares that it will "value, actively pursue, and leverage diversity in our employees, and through our relationships with customers, business partners and communities, because it is essential to innovation and growth." The company is proactive in that it holds itself accountable to certain standards for diversity and integrates diversity with other strategic initiatives.

Any diversity initiative short of a proactive program is not real; it lacks teeth and it lacks substance. Organizations short on commitment usually expose themselves in at least one of two ways: inadequate resource allocation and lack of accountability. All too often, organizations don't commit adequate dollars to make their diversity efforts work. Yes, you may attend all the important Unity Dinners and People of Color Conferences. But now that we're being honest, we know this is not real money. This is "make nice-nice" money. Organizations also underpay, overwork, and neglect to develop the skills needed to fulfill the roles tasked with driving the diversity recruiting effort. You don't hear, "Lets not put Mary on that project because she makes too much money" with regard to other important strategic initiatives. So why diversity? Without proper resources, results suffer. But since few results are expected anyway, failure in diversity becomes a self-fulfilling prophecy.

Here's what companies do when they allocate "real" resources to a project: They fund research to study the issue. They fund manpower to create a business plan. They fund a carefully thought-out, adequate budget, and put their most talented people on the project. They pay them well, give them the tools they need to succeed, and incent them to deliver the best possible results. They monitor progress by measuring intermediate and long-term outcomes. And if the team doesn't deliver, they lose raises, or promotions—or their jobs.

Like many large organizations, Wachovia Bank has a developed diversity strategy; but unlike most organizations, it demonstrates true commitment to the outcomes and so developed metrics to measure progress. The company identified key factors of its corporate goal of increased workforce diversity, and began evaluating recruiters on the completion of these goals, offering incentives for those who presented a diverse slate of successful candidates. The "scorecard" criteria included number of hires, time to fill, percentage of diverse candidates, percentage of diverse hires, interview-to-offer ratio, and offer-to-acceptance rate (Garvey, Charlotte. "The Next Generation of Hiring Metrics," *HR Magazine*, Vol. 50, No.4, April 2005).

This kind of accountability is the other clear index of commitment. It boggles my mind how people can sit at a big conference table and talk about how they "can't" find any diverse professionals, and everyone else just passively nods in agreement. In the real world, where there is commitment, there are tangible, meaningful consequences for those who fail.

For example, when a consumer product company launches a new brand, a team of very smart professionals methodically conducts market research until it knows where consumers in its target market live, how much money they have, what cars they drive, and what they eat for breakfast. If that team came back and said, "We just can't find any information about our target market," there would be serious consequences. The team members' superiors would question their every move, trying to determine what went wrong and whose fault it was.

These same questions should be asked of recruiters, HR professionals, or executives who say they "can't find any" diverse professionals. Are we really to believe that these same companies that can dig up information on anyone, anywhere, can't tell you where to find African-American accountants or Latino lawyers or Asian-American marketing professionals? Am I the only one having a hard time with this logic? Did anyone ever think that the same methodologies that led a company to open restaurants in Toledo and Santa Fe also could inform us that Xavier University in Louisiana graduates more African-American biology majors than any other university in the country, and has for twenty years (Isaac Black, *African American Students' College Guide* [Wiley, 2000])?

I believe that's called a trend—and it's easy to spot with a little research.

So the first step is to come clean, admit you have committed inadequate resources or failed to require accountability, then strip away the excuses that have enabled you to fail for so long. I don't care what your excuses are; in my eighteen years working in the corporate world and my eight years as a recruiter, I've heard them all, and they are almost always lame. While there are as many excuses for diversity failures as there are companies to make them, the following are the excuses I've heard most often:

1. **"We can't find any."** Well, you won't find any if you don't look. They are out there. Forget anything you've heard about the numbers of diverse job candidates shrinking. As with any statistical analysis, you must ex-

amine the numbers you read with care—and the reality is that every year there are more qualified diverse candidates, not fewer. For example, while it is true that the percentage of accountants who are diverse has been shrinking in the past few years, the overall pool of accountants is growing—so the aggregate number of diverse accountants is actually larger today than it was several years ago.

But these numbers shouldn't matter to you anyway. The issue is not whether there are enough diverse candidates to go around to every organization. The issue is whether you can attract and recruit enough for your organization. This is called competing for resources—something your organization likely does every day. If the challenge were to find new clients, your organization would scour markets and databases, conduct focus groups, and generally do whatever was necessary to find them. Research is powerful stuff—it can reveal down to the street who lives where, how much they make, what they read. But when it comes to diversity, these principles often are not applied. No, when it comes to diversity, organizations run ads in the same old newspapers, attend the same old conferences, and wonder why nothing happens.

Now let's think about what would happen if you applied the same targeted efforts that have worked on other initiatives. Imagine, for example, what would happen if you Googled "accountant" and "Howard University" (one of the leading historically black universities in our country). The names and networking contacts that come up will be largely African-American. Or even better, search for the "Top Fifty African-American accountants" on Lexis-Nexis. If you still "can't find any" after you've called everyone in the results list, and everyone they recommend, and everyone *they* in turn recommend, I might actually believe that you can't find any. But it won't happen. You'll end up with so many candidates you won't know where to begin.

These methods probably sound elementary to you—even insultingly basic—but lots of folks have never tried them. Trust me: to this day I am still meeting with organizations that have never taken these basic steps forward. I have loaded the second part of this book with similar ideas to help you find the people you are looking for. These tactics are as simple as those I've mentioned above, and they work.

2. **"Our search firm didn't bring us a diverse slate."** Okay—so fire it. What would you do if you were trying to recruit a new CFO, and your recruiting firm brought you nothing but marketing people? There are many excellent recruiting firms out there today that can provide you with more diversity talent than you'll know what to do with. You just have to hire them. Again, this is about business logic. Your search firm didn't find any because it didn't really look; it was paralyzed by the same excuses that paralyze you. The reality is, like most organizations, traditional search firms rely on their formal and informal networks to source candidates—and these networks have historically been bereft of diversity professionals. So when you are seeking a diverse pool, these firms are not much help; they

are more likely to reinforce your paralysis. Find a recruiting firm with strong connections to diverse communities, and you will have all the talent you need. The resources in this book will help you get started.

3. **"Diversity candidates just don't make it through the hiring process."** This excuse is a corollary to "We can't find any." If your diversity candidates aren't competitive, it is likely because whoever selected your candidates has settled in terms of fit and job qualifications rather than spending the extra time to find highly qualified diversity candidates. But they're out there, and it's your job to find them. You've got to get rid of the idea that to hire a diversity professional is to lower your standards or to somehow settle. If candidates aren't making it through the process, go find better ones. That's what you would do with majority candidates, right? Of course, there's always the chance that the issue is with your hiring managers, whose biases are preventing diversity candidates from making it through. If this is the case, get real about it. By putting a greater number of highly qualified diversity candidates through your process, you will either move your numbers or very quickly discover that you have hiring managers with active biases. Either way, you'll have the solution to moving your numbers.

4. **"Diversity doesn't affect us."** This is the "Every building in this area will be destroyed by the 9.5 Richter scale earthquake but not ours because we built ours differ-

ently" argument. With people of color in the United States currently numbering 100 million and that population growing rapidly, it is only a matter of time before this explosion impacts every organization's customers and workforce (Jon Meacham, "The New Face of Race," *Newsweek,* September 18, 2000). For some organizations—hospitality firms or consumer goods manufacturers, for example—the wave has already hit. For others—such as financial services and technology firms—the wave is further offshore but still approaching like a tidal wave. No matter which category you are in, you must have a plan and act aggressively. If you don't, you will lose customers, talent, money, and market share. If this sounds like a breach of fiduciary duty—well, it just might be.

5. **"Diverse professionals don't want to work here—there is no one here like them."** This is circular logic and a self-fulfilling prophecy. If you tell yourself this convincingly enough, you'll never even try to recruit any diverse professionals. Of course it's true that some people don't want to be "the only one" in a sea of something different. But from working with and talking to diverse professionals over the last fifteen years, experience tells me that this is far from the predominant view. The majority of diverse professionals I've worked with will work anywhere for the right opportunity.

I certainly don't profess to speak for all minority professionals, but I will say that most of the diverse professionals I know long ago accepted the fact that to make it, they would have to adapt, at least at some level, to majority culture. Being the only one is not ideal—everyone feels more comfortable around people like them—but it is not usually a blocking issue. It is no surprise, however, that majority professionals underestimate this willingness on the part of diverse professionals to work outside their comfort zones, because most majority professionals have never had to make that choice.

6. **"We don't have the resources."** This is corporate-speak for "Diversity isn't that important." When you don't have enough resources to achieve a goal, you are really saying the goal isn't a high enough priority for your organization to fund it. Maybe that's the right call for you. Maybe not. But let's at least be real about it. When Staples CEO Ronald Sargent wanted to recruit more minorities, he knew that the effort would require more than just lip service. He also realized that casting as wide a net as possible would bring in some winning candidates and some that wouldn't make the cut. So he approved temporary funding for more than fifty college students, who worked at the company for a trial period. At the end of the trial period, many students landed permanent jobs. Thus, Staples was able to adjust its recruiting strategies to align more closely with its stated commitment to diversity: "To understand why diversity is so important to us, you don't have to look farther than your nearest Staples store. Our customers—whether they're shopping in our stores, online, or through Staples Contract or Business

Delivery—are a mosaic of different cultures, ethnicities, genders, and ages. So it's not surprising that we strive for a workforce and a supplier network that reflect the diverse multicultural 'face' of our customers" ("Our Commitment to Diversity," www.staples.com/sbd/content/about/diversity/index.html).

Take a look at what your company is funding for diversity. Is this the proper allocation of resources to prepare your company for the next fifty years? If so, I'll buy this excuse. If not, you've got some work to do in reassessing priorities and reallocating resources. The point is, you can't use this excuse unless you've actually done the homework and factually determined that your limited resources are better spent elsewhere. Do that, and at least you are exercising sound business judgment.

7. **"We hired a diverse senior executive, but that hasn't moved the numbers at all."** Well, no kidding. Senior executives do very little hiring, so they are not in a strong position to impact the complexion of your workforce. Also, the idea that a figurehead minority will somehow move numbers is greatly misguided. Managers will not be inspired to hire more Asian people by seeing an Asian general counsel. And candidates won't necessarily come to your company just because you've got a prominent minority executive. In fact, that strategy could backfire because you could be telegraphing the idea that your commitment to diversity stops at window dressing. If you want your numbers to move, hire

diverse middle managers. I'll talk more about this strategy later in the book—it's logical, and it works.

8. **"Our hiring managers won't cooperate."** I love this one. Another classic example of the suspension of business logic. Does the word "insubordination" mean anything to you? The only reason managers don't do anything is because there is no consequence if they don't. Make their compensation depend on achievements in diversity hiring, and you'll see changes. Make promotions turn on hitting diversity numbers, and you'll get results. This is not new stuff—you've got to motivate your people to achieve results, as with any other strategic initiative.

9. **"We only promote from within."** To say that you are committed to building diversity but only hire from within is a joke. These two priorities are directly at odds. It's like saying you are committed to growing flowers, but have a policy against planting things. It can't be both ways. So decide which priority is most important, and move on. Once this decision is made, the rest can be sorted out.

10. **"We made a mistake by promoting a lot of minorities too soon, before they were ready."** Since when does a successful organization quit after stumbling? Again, suspension of business logic. If it didn't work, figure out why, address the legacy issues, and try again and again until you succeed. Minorities are successfully promoted

every day. So you've got to look at whom you promoted and why it didn't work. Were there cultural issues? Address them through training. Was there a mismatch between job and skills? A problem with fit? Maybe the problem lies at the root of your diversity program—maybe you are not trying hard enough to find the right candidates, and are settling because you have bought the excuse that you just can't find any. This book will help you resolve the problem of finding and attracting the right people for the right jobs. When you have done everything in this book, and have successfully built your bench of diversity talent, you should never again have to promote someone too soon.

11. **"We did diversity training and nothing happened."** Diversity training will help create an environment that is welcoming to diversity, but it won't drive numbers. You must give your hiring managers the tools to effect change. The key to driving diversity numbers is to recruit large numbers of highly qualified diversity candidates. Training without a strong recruiting program is like buying a great new lawn mower without gas—it goes nowhere.

12. **"We have run ads and attended job fairs, but nothing has happened."** The key to finding great candidates is to build ongoing relationships. It's all about networking—about reaching out beyond the comfort zone of your traditional networks and getting to know different people. Think about where the nondiverse talent in your organization came from. Did you find most of those

people by running ads and attending job fairs? Probably not. In fact, I bet you found most of them through word-of-mouth networking. So if you are not tapped into diverse networks, you will never get enough diverse candidate referrals. Much of this book will discuss this issue of disconnected networks, and will offer practical, step-by-step strategies for using the power of networking to drive your diversity initiative.

13. **"Diversity results are not measurable, so there's no way to really know if we're succeeding."** This one just baffles me. There may not be the equivalent of a Financial Accounting Standards Board (FASB) standard for measuring diversity results, but there is always a way to tell if you are meeting your goals. You said you were going to hire three people of color this quarter. Did you? You said you were going to recruit at five highly diverse universities this fall. Did you? You get the picture. Or is the problem that you never set any goals in the first place? It is important to note that I'm not using the word "goals" as a synonym for "quotas" in the workforce. I'm trying to drive home the point that setting tangible, attainable, but challenging goals for your company is essential to measuring success.

14. **"We don't have the time or resources to train a bunch of new people."** There is a myth out there that diversity candidates are less educated and less experienced than majority candidates, and so will require costly training. This is complete nonsense, and goes back again to that weak "We can't find any" excuse. If you take the time

to hire qualified diversity candidates, you will spend no more resources training them than on anyone else.

Now that we've identified the most common excuses used to paralyze diversity initiatives, it's time to strip them away once and for all. The following action plan will take you through a "get-real" audit for your own organization. Take the time you need to work through these steps. Once you've stripped away your disabling excuses, you'll be ready to move on to building a productive, successful diversity recruiting program, and growing your business.

ACTION PLAN
Strip Away the Excuses

1.   Does your organization believe it "can't find any" qualified diverse professionals? If so, what is this belief based on? How hard is your company really trying?

_____

_____

_____

_____

_____

_____

2.   If your organization relies on search firms to find diverse candidates, evaluate how well your search firms are doing. What excuses do they give you for not finding more diverse candidates? Has your company

looked into hiring a firm that specializes in diversity recruiting? If not, why not?

_____

_____

_____

_____

_____

3. Are you having trouble with candidates making it through the hiring process? If so, have you researched what is causing the difficulty? Is it because you have settled on less-qualified candidates in the first place? Or could it be that you have discrimination issues internally? What excuses has your organization been using to explain why diverse professionals don't fare well in your interview process? Are any of these excuses supported by facts?

_____

_____

_____

_____

_____

4. Does your organization believe that diversity is important? If not, is this conclusion based on a study or other empirical evidence, or is it just an excuse?

_____

_____

_____

_____

_____

5.   Does your organization believe that "diverse profes-
     sionals don't want to work here"? If so, what is this
     conclusion based on? Has your organization ever
     studied why diverse professionals do not want to
     work at your organization? If not, why not? Is there
     anything that would prevent you from doing such a
     study now?

_____

_____

_____

_____

_____

_____

6.   Is the lack of resources hindering your diversity initia-
     tive? What has been done, if anything, to gain additional
     resources? What is your company funding instead of di-
     versity? Was this funding decision based on empirical ev-
     idence?

_____

_____

_____

_____

_____

_____

7.   Has your organization tried to diversify by hiring di-
     verse senior managers, with little success? Are these se-
     nior managers in a position to effect change by hiring
     other employees? If not, why doesn't your organization

focus more on placing diverse professionals into hiring manager positions?

_____

_____

_____

_____

_____

8. Is your diversity initiative being stalled by uncooperative hiring managers? What is your company doing about this lack of cooperation? If nothing, why? Suggested addition or substitution: Does your organization offer results-driven incentives or consequences for diversity hiring? If not, why not?

_____

_____

_____

_____

_____

9. Does your company have a "promote from within" policy? Has the direct conflict between this policy and your diversity initiative ever been articulated to and evaluated by the decision makers in your company? If not, why not? If so, what conclusions were drawn and why?

_____

_____

_____

_____

_____

10. Is your company allowing past diversity hiring mistakes to prevent progress? If so, why? What can you do to overcome those mistakes and push forward?

_____

_____

_____

_____

_____

11. Has your organization been discouraged by its diversity training results? Do the decision makers in your organization understand that training does not drive numbers, but recruiting does? What can you do to make this point known?

_____

_____

_____

_____

_____

12. Has your organization been discouraged by its recruiting efforts to date? Have you made proactive efforts to build ongoing relationships with diverse networks, or have you been attending the same old job fairs? Could you be doing more?

_____

_____

_____

_____

_____

13. What is your organization doing, if anything, to measure diversity? If nothing, how or why was this decision not to measure diversity made?

_____

_____

_____

_____

_____

_____

14. Does your organization make the assumption that diverse employees will require more costly training? If so, is this assumption based on any empirical evidence? If your company has had to spend more on training new diverse employees, was it because you settled for less-qualified candidates?

_____

_____

_____

_____

_____

_____

2

OUTLINE YOUR BUSINESS CASE FOR DIVERSITY

N ow that you've stripped away your excuses, you're ready to begin building a successful diversity initiative. To do so, you'll need to secure adequate resources. Now let's be honest here—most organizations with tight budgets and demanding shareholders do not commit resources to "nice-to-have" initiatives. Nice-to-have initiatives may get lip service, but they don't get the real resources required for success. Therefore, to secure the resources you need, you must first elevate your organization's diversity initiative from "nice-to-have" to "have-to-have" status. The most effective way to do this is to tie diversity to your organization's bottom line.

The business case for diversity has become overwhelming over the last decade.

In fact, many of the Global 1000 have publicly acknowledged the value of diversity to their organization. For example:

- Microsoft: "At Microsoft, we believe that diversity enriches our performance and products, the communities in which we live and work, and the lives of our employees."

- Eastman Kodak: "We believe that a diverse workforce and a corporate culture that supports diversity are essential competitive advantages."

- IBM: "IBM values diversity and recognizes the need to capitalize on the skills and talents of all segments of its workforce."

- Ernst & Young: "We want a workplace that is fully inclusive and lets us leverage the talents of a multi-cultural workforce."

- Pitney Bowes: "[W]e clearly recognize the growth opportunities that diversity creates—not only in expanding our market access, but in widening our base of mutually beneficial relationships, especially with minority and women-owned companies."

- Bristol-Myers Squibb: "[The company] embraces diversity in our workforce as crucial to our success as a growing and innovative company. . . . Our future success requires superior talent that represents the best diversity of thought, background, experience, and geography."

- PricewaterhouseCoopers: "We believe a commitment to diversity is the key to unlocking every person's greatest potential. Our diversity is our greatest strength, as it is a business imperative tied directly to our bottom line—the key to our continued success."
- Volvo: "From a business point of view diversity and nondiscrimination in the workplace are crucial. Skill shortages, under-utilized customer potential and improved market understanding are only a few of the more obvious business reasons." (Excerpts from respective Web sites, and published statements on diversity.)

This list could go on and on. The point is that these organizations understand the business case for diversity, and you can bet your competitors do too.

The data to support a business case for diversity is robust. The following points should get your business case research off to a good start:

MARKET DEMOGRAPHICS

- Among Americans age seventy and up, there are 5.3 white people for every person of color. For Americans younger than forty, however, that ratio is 2-to-1. Among children under ten years, the ratio is 1.5-to-1. U.S. Census Bureau, (*Census 2000.*)
- Minorities are now the majority in six out of eight of the largest metropolitan areas in the United States. (Humphreys, Jeffrey M. "The Multicultural Economy 2003: America's Minority Buying Power," *Georgia Business and*

Economic Conditions, Vol. 63, No.2.;
www.universityofcalifornia.edu/faculty/diversity/riverside).

- By 2008, the combined buying power of African-Americans, Asian-Americans, and Native Americans is expected to more than triple its 1990 level of $456 billion to exceed $1.5 trillion—a gain of $1.1 trillion, or 231 percent. This will represent 14.3 percent of the nation's total buying power. (Ibid.)

- African-American buying power will increase from $318 billion in 1990 to $921 billion in 2008. (Ibid.)

- Asian-American buying power will rise from $118 billion in 1990 to $526 billion in 2008. (Ibid.)

- Native American buying power will rise from $19.3 billion in 1990 to $63.1 billion in 2008. (Ibid.)

- Hispanic buying power will rise from $222 billion in 1990 to $1 trillion in 2008.

- Minority buying power is increasing much faster than white buying power, which is expected to increase only 128 percent from 1990 to 2008. When minority groups are included, the nation's increase in total buying power rises to 148 percent.

LABOR DEMOGRAPHICS

- The number of white, non-Hispanic persons in the labor force is expected to fall from 73.1 percent in 2000 to 69.2 percent in 2010. At the same time, the number of Hispanics, non-Hispanic blacks, and Asian and other ethnic groups is expected to grow from 10.9 to 13.3 percent, 11.8 to 12.7 percent, and 4.7 to 6.1 percent, respectively, by 2010. (U.S. Census Bureau, *Census 2003*.)

- By 2010, for the first time, Hispanics will constitute a greater share of the labor force than blacks. (Ibid.)
- Women and people of color will represent approximately 70 percent of net new entrants to the workforce by 2008. Recruiting experts say the top candidates will work for companies that aggressively recruit now—through programs for multiethnic students, affiliations with multicultural organizations, and active campaigns on job sites aimed at diverse candidates. ("Workplace Diversity: A Global Necessity and An Ongoing Commitment"—The Career Advancement Sub Committee of the FCC's Advisory Committee on Diversity for Communications in the Digital Age, June 14, 2004).

RISK-MANAGEMENT DATA

- Job-discrimination complaints filed against private companies with the Equal Employment Opportunity Commission (EEOC) increased by 1.2 percent in 2001 to 80,840, their highest level in six years. While the faltering economy certainly was a factor (particularly in the growing number of age-discrimination cases), there also has been a growing awareness among employees of color, women, gays/lesbians, and people with disabilities that this avenue is available to them. ("Hot Topics: Legal Affirmative Action" http://www .diversityinc.com/public/department22.cfm).

COST SAVINGS

- Companies have found diversity leads to significant over-all savings, especially in recruitment and retention. For example:

  - Nearly two-thirds of college students recently said they believed it was important to work for an organization that values diversity. The data comes from a poll of approximately eight hundred college and university students from around the world who were attending the annual Ernst & Young International Intern Leadership Conference in August 2000. (Ernst & Young Intern Leadership Conference, August 2000; *http://www.collegerecruiter.com/pages/articles/article284.php*).

  - To determine the impact of its diversity commitments on the bottom line, Ernst & Young's Office of Workforce Retention calculated the costs associated with replacing a seasoned employee. "Every time we lose 10 professionals, it costs us about $1.2 million. . . . That's a huge impact on our bottom line, and it gives staying power a whole new importance." (Jim Freer, Ernst & Young Americas' vice chair of human resources, as quoted in: Gitlitz, Josh "HR's Job: Make Companies More Money" *Vault, http://www.vault.com/nr/newsmain.jsp?nr_page=3&ch_id=402&article_id=2896672&cat_id=1124*)

This data suggests several key elements for your diversity business case. Through diversity, your organization will be better positioned to attract top talent, improve creativity, improve productivity, capitalize on new markets, build a strong reputation, develop a competitive edge, improve risk management, and operate with greater resources.

1. **Diversity improves your workforce by attracting top talent.** Due to shifts in workforce demographics, if you are not recruiting diverse professionals, you are missing top talent. It's that simple. Without top talent, your company will eventually lose its competitive edge—and its market position. Moreover, much has been written about a shortage of skilled labor over the next few decades. If you further restrict the pool from which you are recruiting by insisting that each candidate fit a very specific mold, you likely will find that hiring has become a costly and difficult task.

2. **Diversity improves creativity.** For most organizations, ideas are the currency of the future. Twenty-first-century organizations will need fewer and fewer people who make things, and more and more people who have bright, creative, forward-looking ideas. If your organization commits to diversity, you will attract the thought leaders you need. The more diverse your staff, the richer your pool of thought, and the more creative your organization will be in everything from problem solving to product development. This will fuel innovation and create a strong competitive advantage.

3. **Diversity improves productivity.** A culture that values differences promotes productivity through increased morale, job satisfaction, and loyalty. Moreover, diversity of thought and skill enables an organization to adapt

and respond more quickly to change, also increasing productivity.

A report by the National Urban League supports this very idea. The study found that companies with effective diversity practices "participating in this study have collectively generated 18 percent greater productivity than the American economy overall. In addition, three-fourths of them have generated productivity results that are in line with or better than select competitors. This suggests, at a minimum, that diversity progress has no cost in productivity, but instead may enhance it, as effective diversity practices are simply good leadership and management practices." ("Diversity Practices That Work," published in 2004 by the National Urban League, available in the Publications section of the NUL Web site: www.nul.org.)

4. **Diversity improves flexibility.** Diversity in the marketplace will require your organization to adapt to a wide variety of ideas and cultures. By diversifying internally, you will create a culture of flexibility that will ensure your survival in the rapidly changing marketplace.

    For a company like Merck, diversity provides a clear competitive advantage. People of every race, every ethnicity, and of both genders need health care. The more diverse a company's employees are, the better they are able to effectively communicate with and meet the needs of their patients and corporate clients. According to the company, "To succeed, we must bring together talented and committed people with diverse perspectives—people who can challenge one another's thinking, people who collectively approach problems from multiple points of view. We will continue, therefore, to cast the widest net in our search for talent—because it is the smart thing to do" (www.Merck.com/about/diversity/employee_diversity/div_competitive_more.html).

5. **Diversity improves return on investment.** Imagine how much you could save if all of your employees felt valued and appreciated. Your turnover costs would decrease significantly; so would your costs for hiring, for training, and for resolving grievances.

6. **Diversity allows you to capitalize on new markets.** Twenty-first-century organizations must adapt quickly to rapid changes in the global marketplace. By increasing diversity in your workforce and supplier base, your organization will be more in touch with customers' needs, and better positioned to develop and deliver valued products and services.

7. **Diversity improves your reputation.** Your organization's commitment to the community matters. Consumers and shareholders around the world are increasingly demanding that companies exhibit socially responsible behavior. A reputation as an inclusive employer will impact your reputation with potential employees, driving down the costs of recruitment and retention. It will also strengthen your reputation with consumers, suppliers, potential business partners, regulators, and community leaders. As Warren Buffett said, "It takes twenty years to build a reputation and five minutes to

ruin it." Make it a goal to be named one of Diversity Inc.'s or *Black Enterprise*'s "Best Companies for Minorities" and you will reap huge benefits.

8. **Diversity improves risk management.** How much have discrimination or harassment claims cost your organization in the last five years? Creating an inclusive environment goes a long way toward minimizing these claims. Not only are inclusive environments less hostile by definition, but they encourage better communication and discussion, ensuring that more situations are brought into the open before they ripen into costly and ugly legal claims.

9. **Diversity creates a larger resource pool.** Through diversity, your organization will have better access to alternative supply sources and new and innovative supply ideas. This, in turn, will ensure your cost competitiveness in the global marketplace. In 2005, Marriott Hotels spent more than $347 million with minority- and women-owned businesses in the United States as part of its supplier diversity program. Acknowledging the benefits of working with diverse suppliers, it also requires its key national vendors to work with minority- and women-owned businesses as well.

Now that you have the facts and arguments that underscore the business case for diversity, it is time for you to begin crafting your own business case. The following Action Plan will help you outline the business case that makes the most sense for your organization.

A C T I O N   P L A N
Outline Your Business Case for Diversity

1. List at least three ways diversity can help improve the quality of your workforce.

_____

_____

_____

_____

_____

_____

2. List at least three ways diversity can help improve creativity at your organization.

_____

_____

_____

_____

_____

3. List at least three ways diversity can help improve productivity and flexibility at your organization.

_____

_____

_____

_____

4. List at least three ways diversity can help improve return on investment (ROI) at your organization.

_____

_____

_____

_____

_____

_____

5. List at least three ways diversity will help you capitalize on new market opportunities.

_____

_____

_____

_____

_____

_____

6. List at least three ways diversity will improve your company's reputation, and thereby its position in the marketplace.

_____

_____

_____

_____

_____

_____

7. List at least three ways diversity will improve risk management for your organization, and identify the poten-

tial impact in dollars saved by avoiding lawsuits and
bad public relations.

_____

_____

_____

_____

_____

_____

8. List at least three ways diversity will impact your organization's bottom line by increasing your resource
pool.

_____

_____

_____

_____

_____

_____

R E C O M M E N D E D   R E S O U R C E S

Outline Your Business Case for Diversity

Books

The Business Case for Diversity. Diversity Inc., 2005. Offers a comprehensive and current analysis of the rationale for and success
of corporate diversity. Purchase at www.DiversityInc.com.

*Creating the Multicultural Organization: A Strategy for Capturing
the Power of Diversity.* Taylor Cox and Paul O'Neill. John Wi-

ley & Sons, 2001. Offers a model for creating a multicultural organization, with detailed examples, an in-depth case study, and discussion questions in each chapter.

Diversity at Work: The Business Case for Equity. Trevor Wilson. John Wiley & Sons, 1998. A hands-on, practical guide to the why and how-to of striving for diversity in the workplace.

Inclusion Breakthrough: Unleashing the Real Power of Diversity. Frederick Miller and Judith Katz. Berrett-Koehler, 2002. Explains how to make diversity a central and profitable part of an organization's strategy for long-term success rather than merely a peripheral program.

Reports and Data

American FactFinder. An excellent source for information on population, housing, economic, and geographic data. Research online at www.factfinder.census.gov.

Bureau of Labor Statistics. A wealth of data and information, especially on the characteristics of the American labor force. Research online at www.bls.gov.

The Multicultural Economy 2005, America's Minority Buying Power. The University of Georgia's Terry College of Business and the Simon S. Selig Center for Economic Growth. An annual survey, available online from the University of Georgia at www.selig.uga.edu.

U.S. Census Bureau. National, state, and county demographic information broken down by gender and race, and special sections devoted entirely to the latest data on the ethnic and racial populations in the U.S. Research online at www .census.gov.

Other

www.DiversityCentral.com. A business center for managing diversity and developing "cultural intelligence."

www.DiversityInc.com. Diversity Inc.'s editorial mission is to provide education and clarity on the business benefits of diversity.

3

SET YOUR PRIORITIES

You have now stripped away your disabling excuses and outlined your business case for diversity. It is time to focus on your priorities. Priorities help you stay focused and on course. Without them, you'll be like a boat without a rudder, going in circles and getting nowhere. Priorities come in many shapes and sizes: there are your job priorities, your staff's priorities, and your organization's priorities. In this chapter, we are going to focus on organizational priorities. Once those are identified, your other priorities will come into focus.

Before you can begin to set priorities, however, you must

first take the pulse of your organization. You must understand what the word "diversity" means to your organization. Begin with an analysis of how important diversity is to your organization. Where does diversity rank vis-à-vis other initiatives? Does it have the same resources as other initiatives? More? Fewer? Is it treated as a strategic imperative, or as something touchy-feely? You'll be able to gather much of this information by looking at the level of resources currently committed to diversity, and the level of executive commitment and buy-in. We'll talk at much greater length about the importance of adequate resources and buy-in in the next chapter, and how to go about getting them. For now, focus only on measuring the current level of commitment.

Next, get a sense of why your organization wants to diversify. IBM chairman and CEO Sam Palmisano issued a statement which says that diversity is an important corporate goal because "the marketplace demands it," and that IBM is "building a workforce in keeping with the global, diverse marketplace, to better serve our customers and capture a greater share of the on demand opportunity."("IBM's Chairman and CEO, Sam Palmisano" http://www-03.ibm.com/employment/us/diverse/50/sp.shtml.) Where did the idea to diversify your organization start? Were reasons given? If so, are the reasons rooted in sound business logic? Were the reasons well researched and supported by the executives in the company? Or were they crafted on the fly, or worse, simply made up to create the image of a company that supports diversity? You probably already have a sense of how to answer these questions from your day-to-day interactions with staff and executives. Take the time now to give a good hard look at these issues by having conversations with a wide variety of people and by gathering whatever cold, hard facts you can find. The roots of your diversity initiative will have a strong impact on its growth over time. It's important to identify and address any weaknesses now.

Once you know how and why diversity is important to your organization, you should take a look at how your organization defines diversity. Diversity can mean many different things to different people and different organizations. It can mean differences in race, gender, religion, sexual orientation, culture, socioeconomic background, physical abilities, age, and thought. It will be impossible for your organization to build and benefit from diversity until you know precisely whom you are targeting, and why.

General Electric's definition, for example, acknowledges "[the] traditional ideas of diversity including ethnicity, race and gender, while at the same time exploring more contemporary concepts like inclusiveness. We track diverse representation at all levels of the organization—by business, by geography and by function." Given the scope of GE's worldwide market, this definition supports its business case for diversity: "As a global Company with operations in more than 100 countries, diversity isn't merely a noble idea—it's the reflection of our business." ("Diversity and Inclusiveness" http://www.ge.com/en/citizenship/employees/diversity.htm.)

If your organization already has a clear definition of diversity, take time now to assess whether the definition is the right one in light of your business case for diversity. If it is not the right definition, begin thinking through the steps you'll need to take to redefine the meaning of diversity. If your organization does not have a clear definition of diversity, find out why not, then work toward developing and communicating a definition that will support your diversity business case.

Once you've identified the type of diversity that will most benefit your organization, you should develop a profile for your ideal diversity candidate. This will help you focus your messaging and recruiting efforts as you move forward with your initiative. What level of education and experience does your ideal candidate have? Where does he live? Where did she go to school? What other criteria might help a diversity candidate sail through the hiring process (e.g., high GPA, professional certifications)? The better you define your ideal candidate, the easier the entire recruiting process will be.

Once you know what diversity means to your company and what your ideal candidate looks like, you'll be ready to start setting goals. You must set goals that are visible and measurable to ensure accountability at all levels, because what gets measured gets done. Any lingering excuses about diversity will wither and die in the glaring light of goals, especially when the goals are highly achievable, and everyone knows it.

Start by assessing whether your organization has already set its short, mid-, and long-term goals for diversity. As with any strategic initiative, it is important that your company have all three. (Apologies if this all sounds too elementary, but I have seen such suspension of business logic when it comes to diversity that I feel compelled to lay it all out.) Your short-term goals tell your team what it needs to be doing today, tomorrow, and next week, and are a great way to measure your success—or identify excuses and failures—as you go. Short-terms goals are like pop quizzes—they measure whether your team is doing its work on a daily basis. Short-term goals might include gathering data on job requirements for the next quarter, or taking the placement officer at Howard University to lunch.

Midterm goals are goals still within view, but far enough

away—in the next year or two—to help you keep your bearings. Midterm goals are like midterm exams: they provide a longer-range goal to aim for, while providing another opportunity to check any paralyzing excuses or failures. Midterm goals might include metrics such as establishing working relationships with the heads of twenty diversity organizations, or establishing successful recruiting programs at thirty diverse colleges and universities.

Finally, long-range goals are like finals: they are the ultimate measure of your success. Be sure to set your goals high, but not too high, or you'll create another excuse for failure. Long-range goals will focus on the numbers your company should achieve in recruiting and retention over the next four or five years. Marriott provides an excellent example of setting long-range goals consistent with its business goals and initiatives for diversity outreach. In 2005, it pledged $1 billion to minority- and women-owned suppliers, and it aims to have its numbers of minority owners and franchisees double in five years. In 2001, Kodak set a goal to have 10 percent of its annual domestic purchasing of materials, equipment, and supplies with women- and minority-owned businesses by 2006. According to Kodak's Web site, the company aggressively reached this goal more than a year ahead of schedule. After reaching the initial 10 percent, it reformulated and disaggregated its goals, and project that by 2008, 11.5 percent of its domestic purchasing will be with minority-owned businesses, and 12 percent of its domestic purchasing with women-owned businesses.

If your company has already worked through its strategic planning for diversity, you should assess whether those goals were set by the right people, using the right set of assumptions and applying the right amount of business logic. As you work through this process, reread the list of excuses in chapter 1, and look for any signs that excuses are limiting the goal-setting process. Are the goals realistic and achievable? Is accountability built in?

If your organization has not already worked through this planning, you should find out why, and what it would take to get the planning done. If planning will be your task, be sure that you understand the finer points of strategic planning before tackling the project. There are many great books on the subject; if your skills need some refining, buy one and read it, or leverage other planning resources within your organization. Just be sure to approach this planning process as you would any other critical business initiative, by putting forth your best, most skilled efforts.

Also, a word of caution: if this planning has not already been done, it may be a signal that your organization does not view diversity as a strategic initiative. If this is the case, drop all your other diversity planning and throw your energy into communicating the business case for diversity. Only when this groundwork is laid will you be able to make meaningful progress on diversity within your organization.

The following Action Plan will take you through the process of setting priorities for your diversity initiative. Please take the time necessary to work through these steps successfully. Setting clear priorities and achievable goals will have an enormous impact on the success of your diversity initiative.

A C T I O N   P L A N

Set Your Priorities

1. Evaluate how open your company really is to diversity.
    Has your company done a diversity study? If so, locate
    the study and read it. If not, conduct an informal inter-
    view of both diverse and nondiverse employees in
    your company. Get conversations going, and see what
    you can find out.

    _____

    _____

    _____

    _____

    _____

2. Who sets the diversity goals for your company? Are
    these the right people? Are they effective? If yes, why?
    If no, why not?

    _____

    _____

    _____

    _____

    _____

3. Why does your company want to diversify? List as
    many reasons as you can.

    _____

    _____

    _____

    _____

4. How is "diversity" defined at your company? Racial diversity? Gender diversity? Age diversity? Religious diversity? All of the above? If you don't know, do a little research—ask a few hiring managers how they would define "diversity." Until you define diversity, you cannot set or achieve related goals.

_____

_____

_____

_____

_____

_____

5. Write down a few thoughts on what diversity *should* mean in your company. Challenge others to do the same.

_____

_____

_____

_____

_____

_____

6. Develop a profile for your ideal diversity candidate. Answer the following questions:
   • **What are the target groups?**

_____

_____

_____

_____

_____

_____

- Which geographical regions must they live in, or be willing to relocate to?

_____
_____
_____
_____
_____
_____

- Which job functions are ideal? (E.g., should the person have prior knowledge of specific computer applications or databases? Should he/she be able to type a certain number of words per minute?)

_____
_____
_____
_____
_____
_____

- What degrees are required? (E.g., does everyone in the office have a bachelor's degree? High school degree or GED? Are advanced degrees required (master's, PhD, MBA, etc.?)

_____
_____
_____
_____
_____
_____

- What kind of experience is required, and how much? (Can you hire a recent college grad, or do you need someone with many years of professional experience? Does the position require prior experience managing large budgets or supervising groups of people?)

_____

_____

_____

_____

_____

_____

_____

- What other hiring criteria are applicable (e.g., baseline GPA, top ten school, CPA, etc.)?

_____

_____

_____

_____

_____

_____

_____

7. What were your company's diversity goals in the last twelve months? How well has your company done in achieving these goals? If your company has failed to achieve its goals, identify at least three things that may be holding your company back.

_____

_____

_____

_____

_____

_____

8.   Write out your company's diversity hiring goals for the
     next six months. If this planning has not yet happened,
     outline action steps to get it done.

_____

_____

_____

_____

_____

_____

_____

9.   Write out your company's diversity hiring goals for the
     next two years. If this planning has not yet happened,
     outline action steps to get it done.

_____

_____

_____

_____

_____

_____

_____

10. Write out your company's diversity hiring goals for the
     next five years. If this planning has not yet happened,
     outline action steps to get it done.

_____

_____

_____

_____

_____

_____

11. How does your company measure success in diversity? We will discuss this issue in much greater detail later in the book. For now, just audit your current practices, and begin thinking about how well they are working.

_____

_____

_____

_____

_____

_____

RECOMMENDED RESOURCES

Set Your Priorities

Books

Action Books: Diversity Breakthrough! Strategic Action Series. Debbe Kennedy et al. Berrett-Koehler, 2001. A series of six booklets. The first booklet, *Assessment,* helps you take a diversity inventory.

Magazines

Diversity Inc. Bimonthly magazine with news, best practices, statistics, and more. www.DiversityInc.com.

Profiles in Diversity Journal. Bimonthly magazine with information on best practices and strategies for diversity. www .diversityjournal.com.

AIRS provides an annual Diversity Sourcing Summit cosponsored by the *New York Times.* For more info, see http://www.airsdirectory.com/mc/training_diversity_summit.guid. AIRS also has resources on diversity recruiting; see http://www.airsdirectory.com/mc/training_drive_diversity.guid.

Multiculturaladvantage.com is an online community where minority professionals and leaders can stay informed, identify opportunities, and learn firsthand what it takes to stay ahead of the pack. Included are thousands of articles, checklists, research reports, and links covering career issues, diversity, racism, English as a second language, immigration, education, business, and other topics of interest to minorities and people working with multicultural issues.

4

GET YOUR HOUSE IN ORDER

Okay. You've stripped away your disabling excuses, created a business case for diversity, and clarified your priorities. You're probably ready to charge out there and make things happen. The freedom that comes from operating in an environment of truth can generate a tremendous amount of energy. But to those of you who would push out there and start recruiting aggressively, I say, "Whoa!" I'm glad you're feeling the passion and the energy—but before you start recruiting, you must first be sure your house is in order. Think of a farmer planting her crops. She can invest in the most expensive seed, drive the most sophisticated John Deere tractor, and apply the latest farming techniques, but if she hasn't cared for the soil—fertilized it, tilled it—much of her effort will be for naught.

After Coca-Cola settled a discrimination lawsuit in 2000, the corporation spent time, money, manpower, and other resources to change the company's direction, and it got its house in order. It has spent more than $800 million on supplier diversity programs, mentoring, and training. In 2006, Coca-Cola was named one of the "Top 50 Corporations for Supplier Diversity" in *Hispanic Trends* magazine. The company also created a diversity vice president position, which oversees diversity strategy, executive diversity training, employee forums, and the company's $1 billion Empowerment and Entrepreneurship program for minority- and women-owned businesses. Coca-Cola elected to slow down in order to speed up in this area, and it is working.

Some of you may now be wondering, "First he says we aren't doing enough, so we start running, then he says slow down. What gives?" The goal of this book is to help you succeed. To succeed, you have to take the time to do things right. There are four issues that require your immediate attention before you rush out and start recruiting:

First, you must be sure that you have addressed any glaring workplace discrimination issues, and have a solid plan to address such issues in the future.

Second, you must be sure you have management buy-in and adequate resources. Without these two things, your diversity recruiting initiative is DOA.

Third, you must be sure that your diversity recruiting practices are shipshape.

And finally, you must be sure that you have reviewed and revised your retention practices, so you'll have a fighting chance of keeping your hard-won recruits. Recruiting without a retention plan is like pouring money down the drain.

Once you've addressed these four issues, you will be in excellent shape to go out and start recruiting diverse professionals.

ASSESS YOUR ENVIRONMENT

The importance of creating a nondiscriminatory, inclusive workplace cannot be overstated. There is no chance that you will succeed at diversity recruiting if you have any overt workplace issues—or any covert ones for that matter. You must address these issues. Don't think you can hire your way out of them, that somehow by increasing the diversity inside your organization these issues will go away. They won't. In fact, they are likely to get whole lot worse—like pouring gas on a fire.

Thousands of articles, hundreds of books, entire industries, have grown up around addressing workplace discrimination. This is not an issue this book can or will try to resolve. If you have workplace discrimination issues, you should put this book aside right now and go create a different kind of strategy. You can't achieve any kind of meaningful success in diversity hiring until these issues are resolved. I've included at the end of this chapter a list of resources that can help you attack your workplace issues. But don't underestimate the enormity of this project—it could take months, even years, to make significant headway.

For those of you who do not have overt workplace issues, I would still encourage you to pay attention to and be sensitive to these issues. Covert issues quickly become overt, and even gossip about events that aren't true can tarnish your organization's image in the public eye—and in the eyes of potential recruits.

GET MANAGEMENT COMMITMENT AND BUY-IN

Management commitment and buy-in are essential to the success of any strategic initiative. Without them, you may get a few things done, but the resources you'll need when the going gets tough just won't be there. When you need to hire more recruiters to do research and networking, you won't have the funds. When your new initiative begins to bear fruit, and you are ready to start that first big round of interviews, you'll lose your budget in the shifting sands of priorities.

Management commitment isn't about just resources, either. It's also about leadership. It's about sending messages to everyone down the line that diversity is important and valued, that success at your organization means successfully playing a role in the diversity hiring process. Many a diversity initiative languishes because it's considered an "HR thing" and not a strategic imperative. Most employees will not go the extra mile to adopt new practices or learn new strategies unless they have to—and they won't feel they have to unless and until they hear from the top that it's really, really important. It's that simple. Consider the following approach from a leader who gets it; Kodak CEO Antonio Perez:

> Diversity and inclusion is a key business imperative for us. . . . To give our top managers deeper understanding, we ask many of them to serve as Corporate

Diversity and Inclusion Champions. In these roles, they interact with, and learn from, Kodak's many cultural and social constituencies. In turn, they become participants in—and leaders of—a dialogue of inclusion. ("Antonio Perez's Message" http://www.kodak .com/global/en/corp/diversity/cpqperez.jhtml?pq -path=7657.)

If you are reading this and you are in management, take a moment now to examine your level of commitment. Be honest. If you are not willing to dedicate the manpower and resources required to win at diversity, if you are not willing to be a leader on this issue, then put this book down, give up on your diversity initiative, and stop wasting time. But if you are willing to make this commitment, do it. Today.

If you are not management, but are working with management as an HR manager or recruiter, you've got to assess where it stands. What is management's level of commitment? How is this affecting the diversity initiative, and what can you do to make things better? This is a complicated topic, and one on which an entire book could be written. My goal here is to get you thinking about the issue, and to equip you with the resources to make things better. The following Action Plan will walk you through an audit of management buy-in for your diversity initiative.

ACTION PLAN

Audit Management Commitment and Buy-in

1. Where does diversity rank with respect to other cor-
    porate priorities? Does the resource commitment
    match up? Jot down your thoughts here, then do
    some research and put together an apples-to-apples
    comparison.

    _____

    _____

    _____

    _____

    _____

    _____

2. Who sets the strategic diversity goals for your com-
    pany? Who sets other strategic goals? If these are dif-
    ferent people, are they at different levels of authority?
    Examine diversity decision making generally, with an
    eye to how much attention it gets from management.

    _____

    _____

    _____

    _____

    _____

    _____

3. Whose names go on internal messaging about diver-
    sity? Do messages come from the office of the presi-
    dent, or do they come from an HR staffer? If

messaging does not come from the executive suite, why not, and what would it take to change this?

_____

_____

_____

_____

_____

_____

4. Who are the diversity champions in your company, and what positions do they hold? Are they effective leaders? Are they respected within your company? Who would be on your dream team of managers to support the diversity initiative?

_____

_____

_____

_____

_____

_____

DEVELOP DIVERSITY RECRUITING BEST PRACTICES

Assuming your organization is clear of any workplace discrimination or hostility and you have secured management's commitment to diversity, you should now focus your attention on your internal recruiting practices. Most organizations model important business functions on a series of well-thought-out best practices; diversity recruiting should be no different. You cannot allow your diversity recruiting practices to be developed on the fly. In this section, I will provide insights into recruiting practices that work. These insights are based on hundreds of conversations with senior executives at major organizations as well as my own extensive experience.

The key to developing effective diversity recruiting practices is to understand the sensitivities of diverse candidates. Because of past experiences, diverse candidates are far more likely than majority candidates to question motivations and envision slights, real or imagined, throughout the entire recruiting process. This not only has the potential to affect your reputation in diverse communities; it can also lead to ugly accusations of discriminatory conduct. It is important, therefore, to craft best practices that are both legally sound and sensitive to the needs of diversity candidates, and to ensure that anyone who interacts with diversity candidates is well versed in these practices.

When developing your best practices, you must start from the very beginning—from the very first impression—and work from there, always looking at your practices through a lens of sensitivity. What do candidates see and hear when they first meet someone from your organization? What does their invitation letter say? What artwork do they see when they enter your lobby? What magazines have been put out to read? Are you all about Norman Rockwell and the *Economist*? Subtle messaging to diversity candidates starts from day one. What would it take to have a piece of East Indian art on the wall, or a copy of *Diversity Today* on your end table? Remember, when a candidate arrives for an interview, he or she is likely to be nervous. Seeing images that illustrate your appreciation of cultural differences can go a long way toward making that all-important first impression of inclusivity. A friend of mine has a child whose pediatrician is very proactive and has an office that is consistent with her commitment to a welcoming environment. The office has five examination rooms, each of which is decorated according to a different ethnic theme: Caucasian, Native American, Hispanic/Spanish, African, and Asian. Wall hangings, children's books, and colorful mosaics are consistent with each ethnic theme.

This is incredibly powerful stuff, but be careful not to overdo it. Diversity candidates can be very sensitive to companies that try too hard, and could well begin to doubt the sincerity of your efforts.

Once you've refined your first-impression strategy, you must thoroughly evaluate the mind-set of your hiring team. Are the team members on board with your diversity goals? Have they been trained to understand cultural sensitivities? Have their personal styles been evaluated for compatibility with diversity hiring? I know, some of you are thinking that personal style is a private thing—something that should not be challenged. But once again, if an issue is impairing your organization's ability to reach its goals, you must address it. If you don't, you are suspending business logic and hastening failure. There can be no "Oh well, that's just the way he is." There must be direct conversations with problematic individuals, and if no changes occur, direct corrective action. If still nothing happens, you must somehow insulate candidates from encounters with these people. The problem and solutions are clear; don't get bogged down in excuses.

For example, Wachovia revamped its in-house metrics plan to reflect an emphasis on diversity recruiting, and getting the HR team on board was a large part of that process. "Recruiters' initial response was not universally positive; some expressed frustration because they had no control over the actual hiring process, [Sarah George, senior vice president of recruiting,] notes. 'We had some good conversations,' she says, and eventually 'the recruiters got to a good place on this' " (Charlotte Garvey, "The Next Generation of Hiring Metrics," *HR Magazine,* April 2005).

Next, you must think through the process of initiating contact, structuring interviews, and, most important, communicating decisions and next steps. Most diversity candidates will have their bias antennae up when they visit your organization. They will be looking for ways that they are being treated differently than other candidates. Therefore, it's not a good idea to have a "diversity recruiting day" when all of your diversity candidates come at the same time, or to have diverse candidates meet only with diverse employees. Diversity candidates want affirmation that you see them as *qualified* professionals more than as *diverse* professionals. Take, for example, 3M's approach to diversity recruiting. Its main focus is on the person as an individual, not a potential fulfillment of an in-house quota. "Recruiting efforts are first and foremost dedicated to identifying talent. With that goal in mind, we look for individuals from all walks of life that share our commitment to innovation and excellence" ("Diversity at 3M" http://www.3m .com/about3m/diversity/recruiting.jhtml).

This can be a fine line to walk—being sensitive to the specific needs of diversity candidates while not calling attention to their differences—but it is possible, and your efforts will pay off.

When it comes to recruiting diverse professionals, communication (or lack thereof) can also be a huge issue. Here again, it is important to remember the skepticism most diverse professionals carry through the hiring process. We can all pretend that communication to majority candidates and diversity candidates is interpreted the same way, but in reality, it's not. Most diversity candidates have a history of being denied access to opportunities, of being limited and judged solely because of their race. While this sensitivity is not often visible on the surface, it does exist several layers down. This means, for example, that when you interview someone but decide not to hire him, you must tell him as clearly, as directly, and as quickly as possible. Do not say "We aren't sure" or "Maybe later" if you know that the true odds are close to zero. Otherwise, candidates will walk away from your organization presuming that they just got the same old runaround.

Another, far more subtle area of communication centers on messaging about the job itself. Candidates will be listening for indicia about whether they are being considered as a potential token. They will be weighing whether the job offers a strategic role with the power to effect change, or a tactical, hang-around-the-office-but-don't-say-much role. Your goal should be to hire as many diversity professionals as you can into strategic roles. In fact, experience shows that your entire diversity recruiting initiative will benefit if you focus your efforts specifically on mid-level management roles. Once empowered, these are the managers who can really make diversity grow: they are the ones who do most of the hiring, and they are the ones with the strongest diversity networks from which to develop future diversity candidates.

The importance of appropriate communication on all fronts cannot be overstated. Every word, every encounter, counts. Each has ripple effects—either positive or negative—because the impression you make on a diversity candidate is the impression you make on his or her network of friends and colleagues. We've already talked a bit about networking, and I will address the topic at much greater length later in the book, but I will reiterate here that successful networking is by far the most important ingredient in any diversity recruiting program. You want your reputation for inclusivity to precede you—to pass from network to network to network—until you become widely known as a great place for diverse professionals to work.

You should never underestimate the power of a diversity network. Word travels fast. If you have an interview process or environment that is perceived to be cold or unwelcoming, the word will spread. Quickly. And you may not know it—until you see the impact in your stalled diversity initiative.

ACTION PLAN

Develop Recruiting Best Practices

1. Do you have a solid understanding of the legal issues that relate to your diversity hiring program? Do all of your hiring managers? Take a moment to jot down any concerns you have currently, and any areas you would like to understand better. Set up a meeting with counsel to review and refine your procedures. Determine who needs further training, and provide it. Also do some reading on the topic to keep yourself up-to-date.

_____

_____

_____

_____

_____

2. Outline your current procedures for conducting initial interviews with diverse candidates. What's working? What isn't? Write out your thoughts.

_____

_____

_____

_____

_____

3. What do diversity candidates see and hear when they first arrive at your company? Write down your thoughts, then identify three ways you could improve this reception.

_____

_____

_____

_____

_____

4. Whom do diversity candidates meet with at your company, and why? What steps can you take to ensure that diversity candidates don't feel like they are being treated differently than majority candidates?

_____

_____

_____

_____

_____

5. Does everyone in HR effectively communicate with diversity candidates? Do they understand the poten-

tial sensitivities and concerns of such candidates? How comfortable are they interviewing candidates? Write down any concerns you have, and brainstorm ways to address them. What sort of training might help?

_____

_____

_____

_____

_____

_____

6.   Do all of your hiring managers effectively interview diversity candidates? Do they understand the potential sensitivities and concerns of such candidates? How comfortable are they interviewing candidates? Informally talk to managers and try to get a reading. Write down any concerns you have, and brainstorm ways to address them. What sort of training might help?

_____

_____

_____

_____

_____

_____

7.   Are there any interviewing managers who do not appear to communicate your company's diversity message effectively to candidates? Are there any patterns you can discern with respect to various interviewing or hiring managers? Write down any concerns you have, and brainstorm ways to address them. What sort of training might help?

_____

_____

_____

_____

_____

8. Outline a plan for assessing and tracking diversity interview results in the future.

_____

_____

_____

_____

_____

9. Outline a plan for addressing issues arising from diversity interviews.

_____

_____

_____

_____

_____

10. Outline your current procedures for conducting callbacks. What's working? What isn't? Brainstorm new procedures to improve your callback process.

_____

_____

_____

_____

11. Develop your internal plan for handling rejected candidates. How will you decide it's a no? How will you be sure that the negative decision is for nondiscriminatory reasons? What kind of paperwork or other information should you gather and keep for legal reasons? Who will manage this process?

_____

_____

_____

_____

_____

12. Develop your external plan for handling rejected candidates. Who will communicate the negative decision, and how will this be handled?

_____

_____

_____

_____

_____

13. How much of your diversity hiring efforts are focused on middle-level managers? These are the managers that do most of the hiring, and will be in the best position to effect change. Brainstorm ways to increase your efforts on this front.

_____

_____

_____

_____

_____

14. List five steps you can take internally to improve placement of minorities in middle-level management positions, and set an appropriate goal.

_____

_____

_____

_____

_____

_____

15. Identify five additional things your company could be doing to improve best practices in diversity recruiting.

_____

_____

_____

_____

_____

_____

REFINE RETENTION PRACTICES

A real diversity initiative doesn't involve just finding and recruiting candidates—it involves keeping them, too. It does your organization no good to spend significant resources on hiring if your candidates just turn around and leave. This is a very real problem with very real, bottom-line consequences. The attrition rate for diverse employees can be three times as high as that for nondiverse employees, and losing an employee can cost four times the employee's salary including costs to temporarily fill the position, find a permanent replacement, and train the replacement. When the recruit is a harder-to-find minority, replacement costs are even higher.

Diverse employees leave jobs for many reasons, but the main issues appear to be lack of demonstrated commitment to diversity; stereotypes that overshadow employee credibility and competency; ill-equipped and ineffective managers; lack of a clear career path or commitment to development; shifting criteria for advancement and limited opportunities to succeed; and cultural insensitivity or misunderstandings.

Fortunately, these are problems with solutions. We've already talked about addressing workplace discrimination issues, securing management buy-in, and improving your recruiting process. These improvements will all help with retention. Companies can also improve retention by reforming certain performance-review and promotion practices, and by starting networking and mentoring programs.

The following performance-review and performance practices have been proven to improve retention of diverse employees:

- **Use a formal committee to make performance and promotion decisions.** This reduces the effect of informal, possibly biased decision-making networks. These committees compile written standards for evaluation and promotion, make sure they are clearly understood, and implement procedures that avoid any presumption of incompetence for diverse professionals.

- **Allow lateral moves.** This improves career opportunities and visibility, and avoids stereotypical roles.

- **Avoid granting special favors or status to diverse professionals.** Special privileges should be granted only in keeping with published rules and standards that apply to all employees. Doing otherwise may reinforce stereotypes, undermine respect from other employees, and foster resentment.

- **Keep the lines of communication open.** Conduct exit interviews, and regularly schedule discussions of issues important to employees.

- **Measure diversity achievements and reward managers.** For example, Pitney Bowes assigns each of its business units a Business Unit Diversity rating, which is then applied when calculating the managers' bonuses. The rating is based on things like diversity representation in front-line supervisory roles and professional and sales positions, and in procurement from minority- and women-owned businesses.

- **Ease new employee transitions.** For example, one recruiting company I know puts a new executive and his/her boss together for a one- or two-day session before the new hire reports to work. In these sessions, each nails down what the other is expecting going forward, avoiding any unexpected gaps between promise and performance.

- **Formalize succession planning programs.** Such programs offer strong benefits to all employees—but especially to diverse employees. Effective succession planning programs typically:
  - Identify the competencies and experiences required for success. Often when the backgrounds of senior managers are analyzed, characteristics that are important for success and advancement emerge. In succession planning, these characteristics can be used as guidelines for identifying succession candidates.

- Require managers to identify several candidates who could fill their position—including qualified diverse candidates.

- **Offer development and training programs.** These programs often include training in leadership and management, career planning, succession planning and development, professional development, and other business skills.

Networking and mentoring programs are also powerful retention tools. A poll conducted by the National Welfare to Work Partnership showed that mentoring had a significant impact on employees entering the workforce:

- 75 percent of businesses reported improved work performance
- 67 percent reported higher job retention
- 63 percent reported reduced absenteeism
- 52 percent found cost savings for their company (marketing materials from Workforce Development Inc., printed from www.workforcedevelopment.ws [September 1, 2002], citing a poll by the National Welfare to Work Partnership)

Mentoring lowers turnover and absenteeism rates, improves communication, increases productivity, and improves creativity. This is another suspension-of-business-logic moment: if you can create a program that improves your diversity numbers, while also improving work performance and saving money for your company, you should do it, right? Citigroup, which landed on Diversity Inc.'s "Top 10 Companies for Recruitment and Retention," states that it works "hard to develop and retain employees. Every year, we assess the company's top talent, and identify women and minorities to ensure that we develop a strong and diverse pool of future leaders. We also help employees develop their careers through informal networking and mentoring. Some 75 percent of our Management Committee participates in mentoring, along with many of our other employees" (www.citigroup.com).

Seventy-six percent of *Fortune*'s top twenty-five companies offer mentoring programs, compared with 55 percent of the companies that didn't make the list (Mentoring Institute, "Proof That Corporate Mentoring Works," www.tmistl.org [May 2002], citing *Fortune,* January 10, 2000). Which do you want to be?

Now, you may be saying, "Mentoring is all well and good, but shouldn't it be an informal partnership that just happens naturally?" The truth is, comfort-zone issues (and sometimes subtle, unspoken biases) make senior managers reluctant to mentor minorities. These same factors also make minorities reluctant to seek a mentor. With that kind of double whammy, the only way to succeed is to thoughtfully and deliberately bridge the comfort-zone gap through a formal mentoring program.

Networking groups can be a strong complement to mentoring, or can stand alone as an effective means of improving retention. Unlike mentoring, informal employee networks are a natural occurrence, especially within larger organizations. (What's that saying about birds of a feather?) Lucky for you, this means you can slide by on this one and simply do whatever you can to support these informal groups. It is enough just to recognize their importance and power and not get in the way. But (and I'm sure you knew this was coming), with a little greater investment of resources, formal networking programs can result in a huge payoff. Networking programs provide a sense of community; improve processes like performance feedback and employee development and retention; and enable the company to connect better with diverse networks.

Networking programs are not without their downsides, however. There can be backlash from other employees, increased internal divisiveness, even concerns about unfair labor practices. To avoid these pitfalls, you should pay careful attention to how these networking groups are formed and run.

Whatever you decide to do to improve retention, just do something. Without retention programs, recruiting diversity candidates is like pouring water into a sink with an open drain. Retention programs make hard-won recruits feel more comfortable, more appreciated, and better directed—and turn them into strong assets for your company. The following Action Plan will take you through an audit of your retention practices and help you identify where you can make improvements.

ACTION PLAN

Improve Retention

1. Look within your own company. Are there any diverse professionals whose career paths are being neglected? What can you do about it?

_____

_____

_____

_____

_____

2. What does your company do in the area of succession planning? What are you doing well with regard to diverse employees? Doing poorly?

_____

_____

_____

_____

3. Identify ways your company can improve succession planning, especially with respect to diverse candidates.

_____

_____

_____

_____

_____

4. What is your company's position on how employees should be evaluated? Is this system neutral, or does it work against (or for) diverse professionals?

_____

_____

_____

_____

_____

5. Identify ways your company can improve its system of evaluating employees.

_____

_____

_____

_____

6.   How does your company decide who gets promoted? Is this system neutral, or does it work against (or for) diverse professionals?

_____

_____

_____

_____

_____

_____

7.   Research mentoring/networking practices in your industry generally. Look also at practices being used to increase and sustain diversity in your industry. Make a note of practices you think might work at your company.

_____

_____

_____

_____

_____

_____

8.   Evaluate the existing networking and mentoring practices at your company. Are they working? What needs aren't being met? Are these practices working equally for minority professionals?

_____

_____

_____

_____

_____

_____

9. Create an action plan to address the networking and mentoring needs of the minority professionals at your company.

_____

_____

_____

_____

_____

_____

10. When your company brings in a mid- or senior-level minority professional, is that person given a discretionary, decision-making, strategic role, or is that person put into more of a figurehead role? If you don't know, establish a plan for gathering the relevant data.

_____

_____

_____

_____

_____

_____

11. List five steps you can take internally to improve placement of minorities in strategic roles, and set an appropriate goal.

_____

_____

_____

_____

_____

_____

RECOMMENDED RESOURCES
Get Your House in Order

Books

Action Books: Diversity Breakthrough! Strategic Action Series. Debbe Kennedy et al. Berrett-Koehler, 2001. A series of six booklets: *Assessment* helps you take a diversity inventory; *Acceptance* shows how to build internal support for change; *Action* helps you launch a new program or improve your existing one; *Accountability* helps you get everyone involved and cooperating; *Achievement* helps you create a plan for measuring and celebrating success; and *More Action* keeps everyone moving forward on the right track.

Coaching and Mentoring for Dummies. Marty Brounstein. For Dummies, 2000. A quick, concise summary of mentoring techniques ideal for the busy manager. Includes advice on diversity mentoring.

The Diversity Advantage: A Guide to Making Diversity Work. Lenora Billings-Harris. Oakhill Press, 1998. Exercises and action steps to develop tolerance and inclusiveness in the workplace.

Diversity Success Strategies. Norma Carr-Ruffino. Butterworth-Heinemann, 1999. Self-awareness activities and real-life case studies to aid in shifting perspectives and teaching multicultural people skills.

Diversity: The ASTD Trainer's Sourcebook. Tina Rasmussen. McGraw-Hill, 1995. A complete training kit developed by diversity experts. Includes program designs; participant handouts; workshop role plays, games, and activities; and assessment instruments and questionnaires.

The Diversity Toolkit: How You Can Build and Benefit from a Diverse Workforce. William Sonnenschein. McGraw-Hill, 1999. Best practices for leadership and communication in a multicultural workforce.

The Elements of Mentoring. W. Brad Johnson and Charles R. Ridley. Palgrave Macmillan, 2004. Concisely summarizes the fifty most important issues in mentoring, with particular emphasis on the corporate setting.

The Employers' Legal Handbook. 7th ed. Fred Steingold and Amy Delpo. Nolo Press, 2005. A useful, plainly written summary of the laws affecting hiring, firing, and everything in between. An excellent resource on all employment law issues, including workplace discrimination and hostile work environments.

Mentoring and Diversity. David Clutterbuck and Belle Rose Ragins. Butterworth-Heinemann, 2001. A more scholarly look at diversity programs, including case studies that explore what does and does not work in diversity mentoring.

Recruiting, Interviewing, Selecting and Orienting New Employees. 3rd ed. Diane Arthur. (*Recruiting, Interviewing, Selecting and Orienting New Employees.* 4th ed. Diane Arthur. AMACOM, 2005.) Takes the reader step by step through the hiring process, offering sample forms, interview questions, and handy checklists. Includes a section on diversity.

The 10 Lenses: Your Guide to Living and Working in a Multicultural World. Mark A. Williams. Capital Books, 2001. Valuable insights into diverse belief systems, and strategies for effective communication and leadership.

Magazines

Diversity Inc. Bimonthly magazine with news, best practices, statistics, and more. Also provides an annual ranking of the
- top fifty companies for diversity
- top companies for African-Americans
- top companies for Asian-Americans
- top ten companies for Latinos
- top ten companies for recruitment and retention
- top ten companies for supplier diversity

Research online at www.DiversityInc.com.

Profiles in Diversity Journal. Bimonthly magazine with information
on diversity best practices and strategies. www.diversity
journal.com.

Fortune provides an annual ranking of the
- fifty best companies for minorities
- top ten employers for African-Americans
- top ten employers for Hispanics
- top ten employers for Asian-Americans
- top ten employers for Native Americans
- companies with largest number of diverse employees
  among the fifty highest paid
- companies with greatest board diversity
- companies with highest percentage of diverse employees

Research online at www.Fortune.com.

Web sites

www.mentoring-solutions.com. A Web site for Corporate
Mentoring Solutions Inc. Contains excellent resources and
case studies.

www.peer.ca/mentor.html. The Web site for Mentors Peer Resources. Site links to mentoring resources and online publications about mentoring.

Examples of Employee Networks

- Microsoft has myriad networking groups, including African-American, attention deficit disorder, Brazilian, Chinese, dads, deaf and hard of hearing, Filipino, gay/lesbian/bisexual/transgender, Hellenic, Hispanic, Indian, Korean, Malaysian, Native American, Pakistani, single parents, Singaporean, Taiwanese, women, and working parents groups.
- Lockheed Martin has several networking groups: African-American Mentoring & Information Network; Asian American & Pacific Islander American Association; gay, lesbian, or bisexual employees; employees with disabilities; and a Latino mentoring network.
- Other companies that have active employee network groups include FedEx, Bank of America, Allstate Insurance, Du Pont, Marriott, Ryder, Baltimore Gas & Electric, and Texas Instruments.

5

REFINE YOUR
MESSAGING

You've stripped away the excuses, created a business case for diversity, gotten your priorities straight, and put your house in order. Now you've got just one more step before you get out there and start recruiting: you must refine your messaging.

It's hard to overstate how important messaging is to your diversity initiative. Whether you recognize it or not, you are constantly sending signals, both externally and internally, about your commitment to diversity. A winning communications plan will position your organization well to compete in the multicultural world. A poor communications plan—or no plan at all—will result in the missteps typical of inattention, ignorance, and lack of true priority setting.

REFINE YOUR EXTERNAL MESSAGING

Your external messaging is what your company does in the public eye. It includes everything from your logo and letterhead to your Web site, ads, and products. Whatever goes out says something about who you are—for better or for worse. For example, not long ago, a large global car manufacturer spent millions of dollars and many, many man-hours creating an ad designed to appeal to minorities. The ad featured a smiling African-American with a gold front tooth. On the tooth was an engraving of an SUV. I swear to you, this happened. How did an ad like that make it through all those checks and balances into a nationwide campaign? The answer is simple: this is the train wreck that happens when diversity is not a real priority, with real resources and real accountability. This is a company that thought it could nail the whole multicultural marketing thing without diversifying its marketing team. Bad move. As you might imagine, a national firestorm erupted around this company, forcing it to confront its shortcomings in a very public way. The cost in dollars was nothing compared to the damage done to its reputation. Wouldn't you like to avoid a similar fate? My message to you is this: The multicultural train is coming. You can get on board with your diversity messaging, or you can crash and burn like this company did.

Thoughtful external messaging will not only keep you out of hot water but also quickly translate into bankable ROI. This is the game of marketing. Organizations spend an incredible amount of resources controlling the way others perceive them, because they know a solid brand means solid returns. Brand strength is that special bit of magic that makes consumers think that a certain ketchup is better than another, that one electronics manufacturer is the top producer while another is middle of the road. Subtle differences in branding can be the difference between leading the market and trailing the market as an also-ran.

I don't mean to bore you with Marketing 101, but I am trying to make a point here. Organizations know how to build brands. They know how to research, analyze, and formulate messages that will be received favorably by their various audiences. Take, for example, McDonald's. It wants to be known as the premier provider of quality fast food. But its messaging to soccer moms—about salads and yogurt parfaits—is different from its messaging to lunch-pail dads—about double Quarter Pounders and large fries—which is different from its messaging to children—Happy Meals linked to cool animated characters. Each group receives a tailored message about what McDonald's has to offer it. If McDonald's talked only about double Quarter Pounders, it would lose a huge piece of its market.

Messaging to diverse candidates is no different. If you aren't thinking about what you're saying to them, you're probably not saying much to attract them. Or worse, you could be saying things, intended or not, to drive them away. If your goal is to grab your share of the diversity talent market, you've got to apply the same thoughtful brand-building techniques you've applied to other strategic initiatives. If you don't, you are once again guilty of suspending business logic. You know that if you invest resources in building a brand with diverse professionals, you will see strong ROI in terms of talent acquisition, and down the line, in net dollars from increased multicultural market share. So you should do that, right?

And you should do other things, too. Messaging isn't about just ads and Web sites. It is also about your actions, and the PR that builds around them. It's about creating and managing the buzz that zips around from network to network—buzz that can either make your reputation or break it. Take, for example, President George W. Bush. President Bush is sometimes criticized politically for being insensitive to the issues of women and minorities, and for failing to champion their needs. But Bush successfully deflected that criticism at the beginning of his administration by taking real action—he named two people of color to two of the most powerful posts in his cabinet: Colin Powell as secretary of state, and Condoleezza Rice as national security adviser. Regardless of the buzz other groups have tried to start about the president, there has always been a greater buzz around these appointments and the commitment it shows to advancing the interests of all people.

It is worth noting here that the buzz around these diversity appointments would have been diminished had they been the more "typical" appointments to posts at the Departments of Education, Housing and Urban Development, or Health and Human Services. In the private sector, this is the equivalent of concentrating diversity hiring on human resources, communications, and community affairs. Like the president's appointments, your actions must send a clear signal that you are serious about diversifying your company at all levels of power and influence. Merrill Lynch, for example, sent a clear signal of its commitment to diversity when it appointed Stanley O'Neal, an African-American, as its CEO. While this fact is not itself broad-

cast, it does not need to be. At every public event, in every forum, the message to diversity candidates is powerful and clear:
"You too can rise up and lead this great corporation. You are
welcome here, and you will be valued." IMdiversity.com and
the *Black Collegian* teamed up for a print advertisement that had
four photos of diverse professionals at the top of the ad, and the
same four photos at the bottom of the ad. At the top, each
photo had a word listed alongside it: "Stereotyped." "Pigeon-
holed." "Underrepresented." "Glass Ceiling." The bottom of
the ad had four different words alongside the same diverse professionals: "Recognized." "Hired." "Promoted." "Valued." The
center of the ad read, "It's amazing what happens when you
find employers who understand the power of diversity. Put the
power of diversity to work for you."

Now you may be thinking, "That's great, Joe, but how do
we begin to understand what message we need to generate?"
Multicultural marketing and PR is, of course, another one of
those topics that could fill an entire book. My goal here is not to
teach you how to do multicultural messaging, but rather to
make you aware of the issues, help you assess the help you
need, and point you in the direction of solid resources.

Your first step toward awareness is simple: just become familiar with your market. Expose yourself to the worlds inhab-
ited by diverse professionals. Read articles about multicultural
marketing. Visit Web sites, read magazines, and watch television programs that target these audiences. Pay attention to con-
tent and themes. You've got to understand the world you are
trying to reach. It is arrogant to think you can simply sit down
and develop a messaging plan for different people without
spending the time required to understand their needs and their

culture. This is nothing new—it's what you would do if you were trying to understand kids who live in the Midwest, or seniors who live in the Sunbelt. You would put lots of smart people who make lots of money on these projects, and they would spend lots of time figuring out the world these people inhabit, and what messaging would attract them in droves.

Once you understand your target market and the types of messages that are effective, you've got to audit your current messaging with a critical eye, and gather the resources to make changes. Effective messaging is powerful stuff; it will work for you while you sleep. Wouldn't it be great to start receiving e-mails and calls from diverse candidates who got your message and felt empowered and excited to contact you?

A very small adjustment in messaging can have an enormous impact. For example, I recently planned a trip to Florida to celebrate a special wedding anniversary with my wife. We had to decide whether we should go to the west coast (Naples, Marco Island, etc.) or the east coast (Miami, Fort Lauderdale, etc). So I logged onto the Internet to research the trip. As I reviewed information and looked at the pictures, I started to receive a message. I noted that almost every picture of the west coast featured exclusively older white couples or white families. Conversely, the east coast pictures showed a melting pot of people. These pictures swayed us to choose the east coast for our vacation—not because of any fear of bias, but simply because we could "see" ourselves more easily in the place that had pictures of people like us. As parents of three small children, we don't get away much. We wanted to vacation in a place that appeared to offer us the most comfort. The net result: we dropped $3,000 in east coast hotels, restaurants, and shops. If this happens consistently on the east coast versus the west coast, it's not hard to see which coast will emerge as the most popular in the next twenty years. (For the record, I mean no harm to the west coast of Florida. I have spoken to many people of color since our trip, and they have assured me that the west coast is quite welcoming. My wife and I intend to vacation there on our next trip to Florida.)

These are the subtle kinds of choices diversity candidates make every day. Maybe they really like what you are doing in research and development or community development or medical research, but when they see your brochures, they view your ads, they visit your Web site—what happens? If they see a sea of white males, they may well think twice about working for you.

The following Action Plan will take you through an audit of your external messaging, and help you brainstorm ways to improve.

ACTION PLAN
Refine Your External Messaging

1. Familiarize yourself with effective diversity marketing techniques. Which ones would work for your organization?

_____

_____

_____

_____

_____

_____

2. Locate two or three articles on the images and stereotypes that are offensive to diversity groups. Make it a habit to begin clipping examples, articles, etc. Unfortunately, these types of articles are featured monthly in the major media outlets associated with litigation actions and discrimination claims.

_____

_____

_____

_____

_____

3. Familiarize yourself with the top three magazines read by the diversity groups you are targeting. How are they marketing to their audiences?

_____

_____

_____

_____

_____

4. Familiarize yourself with the top three TV shows watched by the diversity groups you are targeting. How are they marketing to their audiences?

_____

_____

_____

_____

5. Become familiar with the top three Web sites visited by the diversity groups you are targeting. How are they marketing to their audiences?

    _____

    _____

    _____

    _____

    _____

    _____

    _____

6. Examine the marketing and messaging of each of the companies ranked as being at the top for diversity. Look at their print ads, brochures, Web sites, TV ads, etc. Also look at messaging aimed specifically at recruiting. How does their marketing appeal to diverse communities? Print out copies of things that are especially appealing.

    _____

    _____

    _____

    _____

    _____

    _____

    _____

7. Examine the marketing and messaging for your top three competitors. Look at their print ads, brochures, Web sites, TV ads, etc. Also look at messaging aimed specifically at recruiting. How does their marketing

appeal to diverse communities? Print out copies of things that are especially appealing, and make note of the things to avoid.

_____
_____
_____
_____
_____
_____

8. Gather as many examples of your company's general external messaging as you can. Compare / contrast it to the research you have done. Is there anything in your materials that could be sending a negative message about diversity? Look at everything—words, pictures, context, subtext, etc.

_____
_____
_____
_____
_____

9. Focus on diversity recruiting messaging specifically. How does your messaging compare to that of the companies you have researched?

_____
_____
_____
_____
_____
_____

10. Assess the effectiveness of your recruiting messaging. Have some messages worked better than others? If you don't know, identify the reasons you don't know and brainstorm ways to measure the effectiveness of your messaging in the future.

_____

_____

_____

_____

_____

_____

11. Set up a meeting with your marketing department to discuss creating new diversity messaging or to review the plan you already have in place, and identify areas for improvement. Then identify concrete steps you can take to make improvements right away, and over the long term.

_____

_____

_____

_____

_____

_____

REFINE YOUR INTERNAL DIVERSITY MESSAGING

Like external messaging, effective internal messaging is also critical to your diversity initiative. It can make or break the momentum of your diversity initiative internally, and can quickly become external messaging that reaches far and wide.

Chances are, your internal audience will be skeptical and unsure about what this whole diversity thing means to them. Does it mean less job security? Less career advancement? Having to put up with less-qualified employees? Left unaddressed, these types of questions can lead to an undercurrent of resentment that makes it impossible for you to succeed. Not only will you fail to recruit an adequate number of talented diverse candidates, but the ones you do recruit will flee once they experience the hostility brewing in your environment. The treadmill effect of this turnover will only exacerbate your recruiting challenges, bringing down your entire diversity initiative like a house of cards.

The absence of positive messaging about inclusion also implies tacit approval of exclusive practices. Sooner or later, this ambivalence toward inclusion, or worse, brewing hostility in the workplace, will become known to the outside world. The internal quickly becomes the external—and you know from the previous chapter the power of external messaging to make or break your diversity initiative.

So how do you engage your employees and help them to understand and support your organization's diversity mission? First, and most important, the answers and direction need to come from the top. If the senior executive team, up to and including the CEO, is not reading from the same script, it will be very difficult to gain the full commitment of your workforce. It is not enough to have the standard line in the annual report that states, "We are looking to build a diverse environment." You must have an engaged executive team that takes every prudent opportunity to spread the word that diversity is good for the organization, good for the employees, and good for the shareholders. Management's proactive messaging on the issue of diversity is critical because the power of unspoken messaging can be enormous. If the senior executive team makes it a priority to speak on the importance of diversity and inclusiveness, all the other managers and employees will fall into line. It is an amazing little thing called response to leadership.

Not only should this messaging come in the form of memos and reports, but also in the form of official changes in corporate policy. One particularly effective method is to tie success in diversity recruiting to compensation companywide. I can hear the groaning now—but the reality is that what gets measured gets done, and what you pay for gets done first. There is no greater incentive than to tie measurable goals to compensation.

Now you may be thinking, "But, Joe, our senior executives are very busy. We don't want to bother them with all these things." I understand this, but executives always make time for things that are important. An executive team that won't make time for diversity is broadcasting something very important. These executives are saying that diversity is not a priority to them. And no amount of excusing or wishing away that message will change its impact. If the senior executives of your organization won't collaborate on messaging, you've got to be honest about what this means: you've got a much bigger problem than just messaging, and you need to reread the previous chapter.

We've all seen what can happen when internal messaging goes awry. Take, for example, a landmark race-discrimination case, settled by a large industrial company in 1996. Far from sending out positive messages about diversity, the company's senior managers were openly using derogatory terminology toward people of color. This created a free-for-all environment in which bias and discriminatory conduct flourished. As the subsequent legal action showed, this type of conduct, this failure of leadership on issues of inclusion, took the company down a path with serious consequences. Had the CEO been setting a positive tone for years around building an inclusive workplace, the situation would never have occurred on the scale that it did.

Ultimately, internal messaging can be a very positive force in building diversity and creating a comfortable environment for all your employees. Messaging has the power to build acceptance and create advocates for diversity throughout the ranks. Don't be afraid to reach out and communicate with employees at all levels. I'm not talking about a memo here or a form letter there—I'm talking about putting real resources into real communication. If you make the commitment, you'll be surprised at the results. With the right kind of communication, I've seen fifty-year-old white males turn into the biggest diversity advocates of all. It's your choice whether your employees run with you or run away from you.

Take the time now to complete the following exercises, and you will be well on your way to effective diversity messaging.

A C T I O N   P L A N

Refine Your Internal Messaging

1. Conduct an informal survey and assess the awareness within your company of your company's diversity

goals. Are there any trends you should be aware of? Any negative feelings toward diversity?

_____

_____

_____

_____

2. Identify five ways you can improve positive diversity awareness.

_____

_____

_____

_____

3. Audit your company's internal communications for diversity issues. What problems do you see? Where can improvements be made?

_____

_____

_____

_____

_____

4. Create a specific plan for communicating the potential revenue benefits of your company's diversity plan to the rest of the company—especially to your business managers.

_____

_____

_____

_____

5. To be most effective, diversity initiatives must reflect commitment—especially by senior executives. Have your diversity directives and policy statements come from your executive team? If not, how can you change this?

_____

_____

_____

_____

_____

_____

R E C O M M E N D E D   R E S O U R C E S

Refine Your Messaging

Books

Marketing and Consumer Identity in Multicultural America. Marye C. Tharp. SAGE Publications, 2001. Offers strategies and tools for companies looking to reach out to multicultural markets.

Multicultural Marketing. Alfred L. Schreiber and Barry Lenson (contributor). McGraw-Hill, 2000. Teaches the basics of multicultural marketing using dozens of case studies and actual marketing and recruitment plans.

Web Sites

www.allied-media.com. The Web site of Allied Media Inc. Site lists magazines, newspapers, radio programs, and TV programs by ethnicity and region.

www.DiversityInc.com/Marketing. The Web site of Diversity Inc. Over five thousand resources and articles on successful cultural marketing.

www.multicultural.com. The Web site of Multicultural Marketing Resources Inc. Site includes a calendar of multicultural events nationwide, a bureau for speakers on issues of multiculturalism, a library of multicultural articles, and more.

www.onetvworld.org. Has a multicultural marketing resource center for the Cable TV Ad Bureau. An excellent source of data on ethnic markets.

CONNECT
AND BUILD

6

MASTER MULTICULTURAL NETWORKING

Congratulations! You put in a lot of work in the last five chapters and successfully laid a proper foundation for your diversity recruiting initiative. First, you stripped away the excuses that were paralyzing your efforts. Next, you straightened out the workplace and hiring practices that were limiting your success. Finally, you reformed your external and internal messaging, unleashing its power to help you reach your goals. And now you are ready, finally, to prime the pump and get your supply of diversity candidates flowing.

There is really only one "secret" to successfully recruiting droves of diversity candidates—and it's really not a secret at all. It's something you've known all along and likely put to use every day. It's called networking. This may seem so obvious it hurts— but I'm here to tell you that almost no one gets this concept, at least not as it applies to diversity recruiting. And I'll bet you don't either—at least not yet. That's why you're reading this book.

Networks drive everything in our world. They make things happen by allowing information to flow, and by providing access to opportunity and power. Networks exist everywhere—at your church, in your neighborhood, at your company—and they always (yes, always) consist of people with similar goals, needs, experiences, interests, or cultures. Eli Lilly has eight affinity groups: the African American Network; the Asian American Network; the Chinese Culture Network; the Gay and Lesbian Employees, Advocates and More; the Lilly Deaf and Hard of Hearing Network; the Lilly Ibero-American Culture Network; the Lilly India Network; and the Women's Network. The stated purpose of these groups is to

- "support Lilly values and business goals, including the company's commitment to foster an inclusive work environment;
- provide networking opportunities among employees with a common interest or culture; and
- create learning opportunities for Lilly employees and/or management."

The groups are also active in creating professional networks, recruiting new talent, and training and educating employees. For example, the African-American network sponsors a program called "Leaders Today, Leaders Tomorrow."

Networks are fueled by commonality. If you think about it, your earliest network was likely formed around the kids in your neighborhood, or attending your school or church. Your network was probably expanded by meeting your parents' friends, and their friends, and so on. You may have expanded it even further at college, at grad school, in your first job. That old saying about birds of a feather is really true. We forge relationships with people who are like us, people who have shared the same experiences, who follow the same customs and rules. It's that old comfort-zone thing again, and it's an enormous part of what makes the world go around.

Networks tend to perpetuate themselves, with like gravitating to like, on and on to infinity, unless and until new connections are made. The result is that those who are in tend to stay in, and those who are out tend to stay out. Information, ideas, and relationships are often recirculated within networks like trapped air, going around and around and around. It is no surprise then that the networks that drive commerce and politics today consist primarily of white men, as they have in America since the landing at Plymouth Rock. And therein lies the problem.

If your organization is sitting around the conference table talking about the need for a new senior executive, your senior managers will pull out their Palm Pilots and create a long list of possibles from the networks they've built over the years. These networks are probably based on either shared business transactions or shared personal experiences, such as being from the same part of town, attending the same school, or belonging to the same country club. In other words, these are shared experiences that do not involve much diversity. So if you ask this same group to provide a list of minority candidates, the list will likely shrink to a name or two. This is not an act of willful discrimination (at least not in most cases); it's just reality. White businessmen hang out with other white businessmen. That's whom they know, that's whom they feel comfortable with, and that's whom they'll recommend for the jobs. Thus, your organization ends up with a candidate pool that looks just like its current staff. I call this the network recycling effect.

This happy hour/country club familiarity not only affects recruiting; it also plays a huge role in retention. Most diverse professionals are well aware that he who is best known to management is most likely to be promoted—so the view from outside the in network can be pretty bleak. That is not to say that minorities and women are without connections. They have their own very active networks. In fact, many minorities and women have far more diverse networks because they've had to consciously connect to networks outside their own in order to build their careers. But these diversity networks still remain largely disconnected from the power networks of large American organizations. Thus, there is a whole series of professional networks operating with little if any overlap. Absent any connection between majority and minority networks, the network recycling effect perpetuates the status quo.

The success of your diversity recruiting effort depends tremendously on your ability to connect your existing network to these more diverse networks. The only way to accomplish this is by mastering the art of multicultural networking. The good news is that multicultural networking is not hard. Scary maybe, but not hard. You can build relationships with diverse networks by adapting the same old social and business tools you've always used. The trick is to fully understand the sensitivities and expectations of the group with whom you are trying to network, and to develop a level of comfort in networking with it.

Most people are intimidated by the idea of meeting new people and beginning new relationships. Yet if there's one thing that's even more terrifying, it's meeting a room full of strangers who don't look anything like you. Trust me—I know. I've been the only black man in a sea of white countless times. But I've managed to build a robust, diverse network over the years, and you can too. In fact, I think you will be surprised at how easy it is.

The following is a list of insights and lessons learned from my fifteen years of multicultural networking. Follow these guidelines, and you can't go wrong.

1. Go into any networking event with the right frame of mind. You must understand that everyone there is expecting to meet new people. They want to meet you as much as you want to meet them, maybe more. Your ability to say hello first usually takes the pressure off of them and allows them to relax and engage in dialogue. It also gives you the opportunity to take the lead in guiding the conversation.

    If you are uncomfortable with networking generally, now would be a great time to build your skill set. There are lots of great books on the art of networking, conversation topics, and related subjects. To get you started, I've included a few references at the end of this chapter.

2. Always look for a personal connection with the people you meet. Remember: commonality fuels networks. Look for the similarities in any conversation: where

you are from, your roles, challenges. The ability to establish this commonality will make a huge difference. A key to making these kinds of connections is to ensure that you and your staff are always networking with your peers. Junior people won't network well with senior professionals, and vice versa.

3. At some events, you may need to overcome initial skepticism about why you're there and what you want. To head this off, be sure that everyone on your recruiting team has mastered a quick speech about what your goals are and what you can do for the people you are meeting with. This last part is the key to any successful networking relationship. Conversations about how you can meet the other person's needs always seem to go the furthest. Networking is about give-and-take and enabling everyone's success. If you show a multicultural group that your organization is willing to engage, for example, by participating in group functions or supporting them in other ways, they in turn will help you with your mission of reaching great candidates. They will become your ambassadors to their community. Lockheed Martin, for instance, sponsors more than 150 INROADS (a corporate-focused internship program for high-achieving students of color) interns annually. The company has participated in and hosted INROADS conferences, and this has paid off. Not only has INROADS rewarded them with recognition for a demonstrated commitment to diversity; the program helps Lockheed Martin by giving it a valuable return on investment in the form of new hires. In a press release,

Robert Tucker, vice president of human resources at Lockheed Martin, stated: "[INROADS] gives us the opportunity to assess top talent through internships during the student's college career and hopefully recruit the student following graduation from college. We have been very impressed with the quality of the IN-ROADS participants and the contribution they can make to our business."

4. You may be concerned that you will say the wrong thing, laugh at the wrong joke, or otherwise appear to be ignorant and insensitive to the diverse people you meet. Don't be. While it is completely normal to feel these emotions, you must push forward anyway. When you do, you will find that you are quite welcome in diverse networks, and that for the most part, folks are quite forgiving. When you share your genuine interest in building relationships, others will embrace you and go out of their way to make you comfortable and welcome.

    You may be thinking, "It can't be that easy"—but it is. In fact, most diverse candidates will readily empathize with your fears and will respect you for making the effort anyway, because they've been in the same place many times before. They know what it's like to get a warm, welcoming look from a stranger in an unfamiliar setting. However, you are responsible for being as polite and respectful of cultural sensitivities as possible. The more time you spend networking with diverse groups and the more familiar you become with diverse cultures, the easier all of these things will be.

5. Never go to a networking event without doing your homework and making a plan. If you are going to an event sponsored by a particular organization, you should know who the executives are, what their organizational initiatives are, when they've been in the news, and what tangible and intangible things are most important to them. Ask the person who invited you, or somebody who has been to a previous event. Look the organization up on the Internet. Taking the time to do this will not only make you better prepared, it will demonstrate your respect for the people with whom you are meeting.

   From this information, build your "win-win" plan. Make a list of what you can offer in one column, and what you want to receive in the other. Set goals and hold them clearly in your mind. Determine whom you want to meet and what you want to take away from your conversations. Write out your plan and follow it like a strategic initiative. Do this for every event you attend, and you will get far more from the experience than free cocktails and shrimp.

6. Be careful about promising much and delivering little on your commitments in networking relationships. Rightly or wrongly, diversity groups will likely be skeptical of your promises. This may not seem fair, but it is the result of the many well-intentioned organizations that came before you bearing promises of wonderful relationships, only to disappear in a sea of failed commitments. I cannot tell you how many times I have seen this occur. It did much more dam-

age than if they had simply promised nothing at all. If you want to safeguard your company's reputation and reap the benefits of new multicultural relationships, you must be committed and stay the course. Remember, it is the little things that matter.

7.   Last but not least, you must find ways to take the initiative. Create opportunities to network. Invite folks over to your offices, host a specific function, and bring other executives into the conversation. It is even easier to share your vision with people when you have the home-court advantage. For example, Gannett sponsored a "Mosaic Career Fair" at its corporate headquarters in McLean, Virginia. Although other companies were present at the career fair, hosting the event in-house may have sent a strong message to the career fair participants.

Now, I know what many of you are doing at this very moment. You are making excuses again. You are thinking, "Why do all this work when I can just stay here in my comfy little world and find a way to make connections through clever marketing?" Well, it's true that we did spend a great deal of time in the last chapter talking about how effective and important messaging can be. But it can't take the place of building relationships. You can't just connect with diversity networks by saying a few nice things in a press release. Networks are all about relationships, and relationships take time and effort. But the effort is worth it because once the relationship is built, it will give, and give, and keep on giving. Your new relationships will serve as a conduit for information, and suddenly you'll find your organization is fully in the loop. You will know what is going on in diverse communities, and they will know what's going on with you. The positive buzz your company will get through these new connections will far outweigh any costs you incur in building them.

To the organizations that will try to build multicultural relationships solely though a big media spend, I say good luck. That is like broadcasting, "We've decided we are interested in you diverse folks after all, so you may now begin flocking to us." This is not going to happen. First, it is arrogant to think that you can just decide to penetrate a cultural network that you know very little about, with little more effort than creating an ad campaign. Diverse professionals are very protective of their community. They have worked hard to develop their networks, often with feelings of hostility toward majority networks. They are not likely to respond well to a glib invitation to your organization's prom. You've got to earn your seat at their table as much as they've got to earn a seat at yours. Relationships take time and must be nurtured. They are predicated on mutual respect and mutual benefit. If you are not willing to invest the time to establish those things, you can write off your diversity effort right now.

In the next few pages, I have set forth a step-by-step plan to help you develop and hone your multicultural networking skills. Once you have completed these steps, you will be well prepared to go out and start making connections.

Master Multicultural Networking

1. Learn some new networking skills this week. Buy a book and read it. Keep notes on areas in which you could improve.

   _____

   _____

   _____

   _____

2. Take inventory of the networking skills of each of your recruiting staff. What are their greatest skills? What are their greatest weaknesses? Where are they most comfortable? Least comfortable? What kind of training might help?

   _____

   _____

   _____

   _____

   _____

3. Assess how well your company is networked in diverse communities. Where have you had success? Where have you failed? Make a list of potential reasons for your results.

   _____

   _____

   _____

   _____

4. What diversity recruiting methods have worked best for your company? Which have been the least effective? Can you isolate campaigns or events?

_____

_____

_____

_____

_____

_____

5. Identify the people within your company who network well in diverse communities. Call them and ask them to lunch. Find out what they're doing, why, and how. How can you leverage their networking abilities to help others?

_____

_____

_____

_____

_____

_____

6. Focus on conversation skills. How comfortable are you (or your recruiting managers) with making conversation in diverse groups? What creates the most discomfort, and what can you do about it? To attack this issue, take a piece of paper and draw a line down the middle. On one side, make a list of things that cause discomfort. On the other side, brainstorm ways to improve the situation.

_____

_____

_____

_____

_____

_____

_____

7. Identify which of your competitors are succeeding most at diversity networking. How are they doing it? Ask around and find out everything you can.

_____

_____

_____

_____

_____

_____

_____

8. Make a plan to encourage employees to volunteer in diverse communities. The more time your nondiverse employees spend outside their comfort zones, the better.

_____

_____

_____

_____

_____

_____

9. Make a plan to encourage employees to become more familiar with relevant diversity media (magazines, movies, TV shows, Web sites, etc.).

_____

_____

_____

_____

_____

_____

10. Networking is best done peer-to-peer. Executives should network with other executives, managers with other managers, and so on. As you move forward with your networking plan, identify employees and executives at every level who can lead the networking efforts on behalf of your company.

_____

_____

_____

_____

_____

RECOMMENDED RESOURCES
Master Multicultural Networking

Books

How to Win Friends and Influence People. Dale Carnegie. Pocket, Reissue edition. 1990. An oldie but goodie on the evergreen topic of networking.

Masters of Networking. Ivan R. Misner and Don Morgan, Bard Press, 2000. Advice and real-life examples from some of the world's most accomplished networking experts.

Power Networking. Marc Kramer. McGraw Hill, 1997. A practical and uplifting guide to success through networking.

7

FIND THE BEST
DIVERSITY TALENT

N ow that you've mastered the basics of multicultural networking, you are ready to get out there and meet some
folks. So where are they? Finding the best diversity talent
is like finding anyone or anything else—it just takes a little research. Do you know which organizations represent diverse
professionals? Are you aware that there is a National Hispanic
MBA Association, an Asian Lawyers Association, and a National
Association of Black Accountants? Do you know which colleges
and universities have significant minority populations? Do you
recruit there? Are you familiar with their respective deans of ca-

reer placement? The heads of their alumni associations? Do you know which fraternities and sororities and community, religious, and social organizations are devoted to diverse communities? These are all great sources of diversity candidates. Trust me, once you get started researching, you'll find far more opportunities than you'll know what to do with.

Before you start reaching out to candidates, however, be sure you are straight on your networking plan. How will you reach out to these total strangers and build relationships? More important, how will you stay in touch with them once a connection has been made? The worst thing you can do is start accumulating names and randomly contact people with no specific goals in mind. As we discussed in the previous chapter, you need a networking plan. Make a list of people you want to approach, find out as much about them as you can, determine what you can do for them, and then focus on building relationships and maintaining ongoing communications. Create opportunities to dialogue with your list in both formal and informal settings. The folks you reach out to may never come to work for you, but you will be well on your way to building a solid network that will feed you candidates forever.

COLLEGES AND UNIVERSITIES

There are tremendous opportunities to network with diverse groups at colleges and universities. The most obvious approach is to identify the institutions that turn out the largest numbers of diverse candidates with the credentials you seek. These institutions range from historically black colleges and universities

(HBCUs), to schools in the southwestern United States that have significant Hispanic populations, to schools in northern California that feature significant Asian-American populations. This data is fairly easy to come by. To get you started, I've included at the end of this chapter a list of colleges and universities in which you may be interested.

Once you have identified your target institutions, the key is to develop a networking plan specifically tailored to academia. In the world of colleges and universities, there are at least three constituencies with whom you need to build relationships: the administration, the academic departments, and the student organizations. All subscribe to very different agendas, and it is important to understand each. You may find that skepticism about why you are there is even more heightened in the academic setting. This is because many institutions view their newly minted students as works of art, and take their treatment very seriously. Therefore, you may have to invest even more time in building these relationships than in other settings. Yes, I did say more time; but if it is a priority, you will make the time.

When coming into an institution, you should always alert the administration and relevant academic departments that you would welcome the opportunity to meet and discuss their initiatives. Better yet, do your homework and come armed with ideas of how you can partner to help them reach their published goals. Schools are always in need of resources—money, equipment, scholarships, books, research funds, internships. If you do your homework, you should be able to develop an action plan that will dazzle your audience. Remember: leading with what you can do for someone else, rather than with what they can do for you, will always serve you well.

When approaching student organizations, be sure to research each group's motivation and track record on campus. This is where one of your new friends in the administration or academia can be very helpful. Your best bet is to coordinate any major student-group outreach through the administration.

Finally, you should be focused on two of the greatest sources of opportunity on campus: the career center and the alumni association. I can hear the "duhs" right now—but here is my response: How many relationships do you have with career-center directors at heavily minority schools? I don't mean the "Let me refresh your memory as to who I am" type of relationship, but the real kind, where they recognize your voice midway through your first sentence. Career-center directors can be incredibly helpful to your cause—not only because they know all the students looking for jobs, but because they field calls from their alumni out in the workforce all the time. When people are transitioning between jobs, they will often reach back to their alma maters for assistance. Wouldn't it be great if they sent folks with the right skill sets directly to you?

Alumni associations are another tremendous resource. Institutions have been graduating talented people of color for a long, long time, and their alumni participate in vast professional networks. Once you begin to tap into these networks, you will have more candidates than you know what to do with.

The following Action Plan will help you recruit diversity candidates more effectively at colleges and universities.

A C T I O N   P L A N

Recruiting Diversity Candidates at Colleges and Universities

1. Evaluate your diversity hiring records and identify the schools from which your company has had the most success hiring diversity candidates. Research recruiting events, career and diversity professionals, and minority professors at these schools. Establish a plan to network with them. Ask for referrals.

    _____

    _____

    _____

    _____

2. Familiarize yourself with the list of historically black colleges and universities (HBCUs). Learn what is special about each.

    _____

    _____

    _____

    _____

3. Research and identify the HBCUs that are the geographically closest to your company or your company's hiring areas.

    _____

    _____

    _____

    _____

4. Research and identify the HBCUs that have the strongest degree programs in areas relevant to your company.

_____

_____

_____

_____

_____

_____

5. From steps 2–4, you should now have a list of HBCUs that are (1) relevant by geography and (2) relevant by degree program. Using this list of schools, compile a list of their recruiting events and programs.

_____

_____

_____

_____

_____

_____

6. Identify the dean of career services or outplacement at the relevant HBCUs. Bring these people into your network. Send them information on your diversity program today. Put their names on your company's mailing list. Make plans to call each of them individually, and take those who are close by to lunch.

_____

_____

_____

_____

_____

7. Research professors in related degree programs at the relevant HBCUs. Establish a plan to network with them. Ask for referrals.

_____
_____
_____
_____
_____
_____

8. Research schools nationally that have strong diversity populations. Determine which schools are a fit with your diversity objectives.

_____
_____
_____
_____
_____
_____

9. Research recruiting events, career and diversity professionals, and minority professors at these schools. Establish a plan to network with them. Ask for referrals.

_____
_____
_____
_____
_____
_____

10. Start a networking calendar. Fill in all of the recruiting events your company could attend.

_____

_____

_____

_____

_____

_____

11. Research the alumni affiliations of the minority professionals in your company. You can draw great recruiting insights from the folks who attended a given school.

_____

_____

_____

_____

_____

_____

12. Identify diverse student organizations with which you could network.

_____

_____

_____

_____

_____

_____

PROFESSIONAL ORGANIZATIONS

Professional organizations are another great source of multicultural connections. These organizations are composed of the type of well-educated, capable people of color your organization is seeking. You will likely be surprised at how many professional organizations there are devoted entirely to diversity groups. A primary purpose of these organizations is to create networks for groups of diverse professionals, so they present a perfect opportunity for you to get plugged in.

Connecting with these organizations requires commitment, however. You can't just show up at their events or e-mail their members (though this can be effective on a limited basis). First, you've got to do your homework. Visit their Web sites, and read their mission statements and press releases. Glean as much information as you can about their leadership, their membership, and who's doing what within their organization. Then get your organization involved in helping theirs. Research their goals and objectives and determine how you can help. Contribute to a conference, work on membership initiatives, serve on executive committees. But be wary of getting involved in only social events. It's great to sponsor the evening harbor boat cruise, but you should offset that contribution with another of more weight—perhaps by bringing in a noted authority to speak at another event. Being seen as the enabler of a good time usually won't get you to the level of involvement required to build and sustain meaningful connections. Through the right kind of hands-on involvement, you will earn your stripes and become part of the family, which in turn will let you spread the word about your mission throughout their network.

You must be strategic in the organizations you choose. Don't spread your resources too thin. Get involved with the organizations that are most aligned with your goals. If you can't engage fully, it will be as though you made no effort at all. There is little value in hopping from conference to conference, meeting to meeting. You must spend your time building deeper connections.

Another great way to connect with professional organizations is to network with their leaders. Research who they are, and find a way to connect with them. These individuals are probably leaders in their field and thus broadly networked. Take them to lunch, invite then to speak at a seminar, send them an article of interest—do the things it takes to build a lasting relationship. As always, remember that if you help them, they will help you.

The following Action Plan will help you improve your recruiting through professional organizations.

ACTION PLAN
Recruiting Through Professional Organizations

1. Make a list of professional organizations for minorities in fields related to your company. See the Recommended Resources at the end of this chapter for a list to get started.

_____

_____

_____

_____

_____

2. Identify the leadership of related minority professional organizations. Network with them. Send them an e-mail describing your business and diversity initiatives. Ask them for referrals.

_____

_____

_____

_____

3. List the key annual events for these organizations. Typically, there is a national convention; there are often regional meetings as well.

_____

_____

_____

_____

4. List the events it makes sense to attend and add them to your networking calendar.

_____

_____

_____

_____

5. Encourage your employees to join these organizations— or even better, serve on the leadership boards.

_____

_____

_____

_____

6.   Identify ways your company can contribute financially
     to these organizations. Opportunities range from buy-
     ing ads in their publications to sponsoring conventions.

_____

_____

_____

_____

_____

_____

OTHER NETWORKING OPPORTUNITIES

It is important always to be thinking creatively about expanding your networks. Thus far, we have discussed some of the
more traditional paths to meeting and building relationships
with professionals of color. One of the most important things
to understand about networking is that it is happening around
you all the time. Most of us are programmed to go into networking mode at a specific time, such as at the National Black
MBA Conference or the regional La Raza meeting. But the reality is that our antennae need to be up constantly. For example, not too long ago I was at a meeting with the senior
executive team of a billion-dollar company. The CEO began
speaking about all the things that they had done to make diversity work in their company: the training, the seminars, the
messages from the CEO. Yet he was frustrated because he
hadn't seen the tangible result that he was looking for—a
change in the company's complexion. He felt they had done
everything. So I posed the following question to him: When
was the last time you were at an industry event, saw an Asian-

American woman across the room, and walked across the room with your hand out to introduce yourself? Clearly, he had never had this question posed to him before. My point is that until you are doing everything in your power to build relationships with diverse candidates, progress will be slow. Do you think that that CEO has ever hesitated to cross the room for a potential alliance partner or a big customer? It is clearly a matter of prioritization and vigilance.

As you move through your day, be alert to opportunities to engage people of color. Take churches, for example. As we have discussed, people have a tendency to worship with others who are like them. And most houses of worship will welcome the opportunity to share good news and opportunity with their congregants. Of course, you will have to be sensitive to how helpful they wish to be, but the reality is that some of these entities have thousands of members, and many of those members may be interested in your organization, or may know someone who is interested in your organization.

People also tend to live in homogeneous clusters. So knowing where those clusters are and becoming knowledgeable about those communities can only help. Community events like a riverfest or parade are perfect opportunities to network with diverse groups. As with professional organizations, nothing will help your organization get networked more than becoming and remaining involved. You don't have to live there or give big sums of money. Just show that you are genuinely interested in learning and helping the community to prosper. At the core, we are all the same. We want comfortable lives, blessed with families and friends and careers we enjoy. Your demonstrated commitment to helping others achieve their dreams will be met by a strong willingness to help your organization reach its goals, too.

The following Action Plan is designed to help you identify the networking opportunities all around you.

ACTION PLAN

Identify Creative Networking Opportunities

1. Identify diversity-oriented conventions relevant to your business that are coming up in the next year. Identify those it makes sense to attend and add them to your networking calendar.

_____

_____

_____

_____

_____

2. For these conventions, identify marketing opportunities and opportunities to participate financially. (For example, your company may be able to buy ads in the convention materials).

_____

_____

_____

_____

_____

3. Are there churches in your area with diverse congregations? If so, contact their administrative staff and identify ways you could work together to spread your

diversity message. The church may have bulletin boards you can use to advertise positions, and there may be opportunities to contribute financially.

_____

_____

_____

_____

_____

_____

4. Identify other diversity-related events in which your company might participate—by sending representatives, by contributing financially, or both.

_____

_____

_____

_____

_____

5. Identify diversity leaders in your community. Send them information on your company, take them to lunch, invite them to your corporate events, offer to help with their projects.

_____

_____

_____

_____

_____

HARVEST PASSIVE CANDIDATES
FROM OTHER COMPANIES

Thus far, we have discussed some of the milder approaches to building relationships and gaining access to networks of color. Now it's time to get a little more aggressive. I am writing this book with the full understanding that not every organization can be the "preferred employer" for diversity candidates, just as not every company can be the market leader. My goal is to equip you with the tools to win the diversity game, and to position you for significant diversity recruiting and business success. But diversity recruiting can be competitive, and you'll have to play hard to win.

One aggressive tactic is to hire diverse professionals away from other companies. To do so, your first step should be to start and maintain an ongoing list of people of interest within your industry and related industries. This, of course, will take research and a committed networking effort. You must always have your antennae up for information about talented diverse professionals. Most organizations have Web sites and newsletters that are full of information about who's doing what, and where. Someone in your organization should track these people and keep a live, ever-evolving list using proven research methodologies. Over time, this list will grow to be hundreds of people long. Now that's opportunity!

You must be careful what you do with your list, however; don't develop a mercenary or predatory approach to the other diverse professionals in your industry segment. This can become a sensitive issue and must be handled carefully. There have been instances where aggressive recruiting has led to bad blood. The key here is subtlety of approach. You should not walk around other organizations asking people if they would like a job. Rather, you should focus on building relationships and creating opportunities to build a meaningful connection. Trust me, you don't have to do anything more direct. Nine times out of ten, word will get out in various networks that you are hiring, and candidates will come to you. Of course, as you establish solid relationships with individuals, it is fine to share with them the opportunities your organization has. If you are really in a pinch or pushed for time, you could also have particular candidates contacted by a third party—either someone in another division or subsidiary, or a third-party agent, like a recruiter or consultant. This approach has a certain wink-and-nod feel to it, but in business it is important to follow certain unspoken protocols.

Please don't underestimate the potential land mines that lurk here. For example, I witnessed a tense situation as it evolved in a very powerful industry group of minority executives. One of the more senior members had mentored a younger executive in his company to the point that the younger executive was admitted to the industry group. Then one day the younger executive suddenly resigned and announced that he was going to work for another member of this same prestigious group. That set the telephone lines of many powerful minority executives buzzing. Mind you, nothing wrong was done. There were no lies; no rules were broken. But there was the perception of disloyalty, of one executive making himself stronger at the expense of another. My point here is that this situation could have been handled with more finesse to minimize the impact.

Such quandaries will likely present themselves to you, too, and there may well come a time when you have to pass on a wonderful candidate because, in the big scheme of things, preserving other relationships is more important to your mission. Your goal is to be cognizant of when this is happening and to plan accordingly.

The following Action Plan will help you succeed in harvesting passive candidates from other companies.

ACTION PLAN

Harvest Passive Candidates from Other Companies

1. List companies in your industry or field with large concentrations of diverse professionals. I've included some helpful resources at the end of this chapter.

_____

_____

_____

_____

_____

_____

2. Now that you have a list, create a who's who by researching publicly available information about the leadership and employees at these companies.

_____

_____

_____

_____

_____

_____

3.   Determine how these employees are networked. If they are in your town or area, do they frequent certain restaurants, pubs, or country clubs? Make it a point to go where they go, to do what they do.

_____

_____

_____

_____

_____

_____

4.   Make it a point always to ask people whom they know and whom they might refer to you. Train all of your employees to do the same. After a while, this sort of casual inquiry will become second nature.

_____

_____

_____

_____

_____

_____

HARVEST CANDIDATES
FROM RELEVANT PUBLICATIONS

With just a little effort, you can go trekking through the wonderful world of published media and find many qualified diversity candidates. Remember that old "We can't find any" excuse? This section is going to put an end to that excuse once and for all. Our good friends in the media have seen to that. For example, *Fortune* magazine publishes a list of the "Top 50 African Americans in Corporate America." Niche magazines targeting CFOs, media professionals, the medical field, etc., have all published similar listings. These lists are fabulous ammunition for the next time you are in a meeting and someone says he's tried really, really hard to find a diverse executive candidate but just can't. Right then and there, you can pull out *Fortune*'s Top 50 list and ask, "Have you called all of these people yet? And have you called all of the people that they referred you to?" And so on.

Another great source for diversity candidates is lifestyle publications that target people of color publications like *Minority Business Entrepreneur, Black Enterprise,* and *Hispanic Business.* These magazines are a treasure trove of data. In these pages you will find articles on business, law, accounting, finance, and publishing, most written by people of color who are experts in those fields. You will also find profiles of successful people of color, or see coverage of events that includes pictures of attendees, along with their titles and organizations. Add these people to your network.

I'm sure this seems like the most basic thing in the world, but it's amazing how many companies do not put simple techniques like this into practice. Take publishing companies, for example. I've heard them say they are struggling to find people of color just like everyone else. Now I have to scratch my head when I hear something like this, because I know how much information they have at their fingertips. Talk about suspension of business logic. This is what I tell them: Ever heard of a masthead? (It's the page in a newspaper or magazine that lists the staff.) Go to diversity publications, make a copy of the mastheads, and start networking. What could be easier? It's like having a list of hundreds of potential candidates dropped right in their laps. And in the case of publishing companies, the candidates are even broken out by job function!

All of this simplicity may be a little too close for comfort. But that's what this book is about—clearing the fog that diversity seems to bring into an organization and attacking problems like with any other strategic imperative. Bring in smart people, give them the resources, hold them accountable, and get out of their way. The rest can be as easy or as difficult as you want it to be.

The following Action Plan will help you succeed in harvesting candidates from publications.

ACTION PLAN

Harvest Candidates from Relevant Publications

1. Identify diversity-focused periodicals relevant to your industry. Read them regularly, making note of any people of interest from the masthead, the pictures, the articles, or the authors.

2.   Network with these people of interest. Give them a call, invite them to lunch, or send them information about your company.

_____

_____

_____

_____

_____

_____

3.   Research which diversity publications it may make sense to use for placing job ads.

_____

_____

_____

_____

_____

_____

FIND CANDIDATES ONLINE

If there was ever a trump card to be played in the game of recruiting, it is mastery of the Internet. Thanks to the flood of information unleashed by the World Wide Web, you can pretty much find anybody, anywhere, anytime by going online. Now I've got to warn you—this section is pretty dangerous. If you're still holding on to a shred of your belief that "you just can't find any," you're about to lose your grip.

When you think of the Internet and recruiting, your first thought probably goes to the expensive job sites. Yes, they are helpful, and I will talk about them in a bit. But actually, the most powerful use of the Internet for recruiting is completely free. You know those Google and Yahoo! searches you run when you need to find a restaurant in Denver or a caterer for an event in Cincinnati? You can use the same approach to find candidates. It's all about mastering the key search terms— punch in the right terms, and out comes an endless stream of diversity candidate leads.

You already know that if you type in the word "restaurant," you will get a zillion references to restaurants of every size and variety in every town all over the world. The key to an effective search is to use the right parameters. When searching for diversity candidates, these parameters are painfully obvious. I've already thrown out dozens of them in this section—names of HBCUs and other universities, diversity professional organizations, fraternities and sororities, minority scholarships, churches, publications, and so on. Any of these terms can be input as keywords to bring back information on people, organizations, and events relating to diverse professionals. For example, if you type in "Howard University and accountant," you'll get any number of leads relating to African-American accountants. Similarly, if you type in "Hispanics and banking," you'll get scores of leads on Hispanic bankers and their networks.

You can also use online searches to track down information on a person named in a picture. Just type in the name and any other identifying information you may have, and away you go. Because Google.com allows you to search for images, you can also do this in reverse—look for pictures of people to confirm that they are diverse. Of course, you won't be able to find a picture of everyone, but this is a great trick when researching executives, board members, or other prominent candidates.

Beyond the free resources on the Internet are the fee-based databases. Type in "top Asian Americans" on Lexis-Nexis and you will be busy for days. You should also be familiar with the myriad online job boards for diverse professionals, such as LatPro.com, IMdiversity.com, DiversityInc .com, and BlackPlanet.com. You can post jobs on these sites and harvest résumés from them, most of them for a fee. You can also apply the search parameters we discussed above to big job sites like Monster.com and HotJobs.com. For example, go to one of these diverse job boards and type in the search term "National Bar Association," and you should get almost exclusively the résumés of African-American lawyers. Remember when you are searching that the key is not just to find people who can perform exactly the role you are looking for, but also to find people who might be in that perfect candidate's network.

With so much information on the Internet, you will have to be diligent and precise to avoid being overwhelmed by your search results. Too much information can be as bad as too little information, unless you have a strategy for winnowing it down. But this challenge should be no different from any other—once, again, it's just a question of resources. If you can't do it yourself, leverage your access to the corporate research department, or find a vendor with this type of research expertise. Remember: no excuses, just results.

The following Action Plan will help you source diversity candidates from the Internet.

A C T I O N   P L A N

Find Candidates Online

1. Sharpen your Internet research skills generally. Learn to use search engines effectively. What training could help you and your team?

_____

_____

_____

_____

_____

2. Have your recruiting staff identify and familiarize themselves with any and all job boards relevant to your company's diversity needs.

_____

_____

_____

_____

_____

3. Create a plan for how to use these job boards most effectively. Will you list jobs? Use them to find candidates? Which boards are the most cost-effective for your needs?

_____

_____

_____

_____

_____

4. Identify the search terms that will return the most useful results. One method is to identify criteria related to the ideal candidate and build a search around those criteria—e.g., "Harvard and Association of Black Accountants (ABA)." Refer to the work you did in the previous chapter on schools, student groups, professional organizations, etc.

_____

_____

_____

_____

_____

_____

5. Visit the Web sites of relevant diversity professional organizations on a regular basis; they will often feature members. Make note of any people of interest, and begin networking with them.

_____

_____

_____

_____

_____

Find the Best Diversity Talent

FINDING CANDIDATES GENERALLY

Books

Campus Diversity Recruitment Report 2005. Wetfeet.com, 2005. Best practices and case studies of successful diversity recruiting programs. Expensive ($1,495) but useful. Purchase at www.WetFeet.com.

Finding Diversity: A Directory of Recruiting Resources. Luby Ismail and Alex Kronemer, Society for Human Resource Management, 2002. Lists more than three hundred places to advertise job openings to diverse employees. Purchase online at www.shrm.org.

Information on Colleges and Universities

U.S News & World Report. Annual ranking of schools, including a ranking of schools by diversity population. Report is broken into different geographical regions, tells you what percentage of the student body is diverse, and identifies the largest diversity population. www.USNews.com.

HBCUs. For a list of, and more information about, HBCUs, visit www.CollegeView.com.

Information on Graduate Schools

Black Excel Newsletter. Provides data on medical schools and diverse physicians. For example:

- Out of the 125 U.S. medical schools, 12 have graduated 30 percent of all minority physicians since 1950.
- Medical schools at Howard, Meharry, and the University of Illinois have graduated the most black physicians.
- Over a third of all minority physicians practice in California, New York, and Texas. (*Black Excel Newsletter, September 2001.*)

Hispanic Business Magazine. Annually ranks the top-ten law schools for Hispanic students.

U.S News & World Report. Annual ranking of graduate schools, including a ranking of schools by diversity population. Report is broken into different geographical regions, tells you what percentage of the student body is diverse, and identifies the largest diversity population. www.USNews.com.

List of Diverse Student Organizations

Multicultural

Minority Graduate Students Association
Multicultural Student Organizations

African-American

African American MBA Association
Association of Black Graduates and Professional Students
Black Law Students' Association
Black Pre-Medical Association

Gamma Phi Delta Sorority

Iota Phi Lambda Sorority

Iota Phi Theta Fraternity

Kappa Alpha Psi Fraternity

National Society of Black Engineers

100 College Black Men

Sigma Gamma Rho Sorority

Zeta Phi Beta Sorority

Latino

ALIANZA: The Latina/o Student Alliance

Alpha Psi Lambda

Hermandad de Sigma Iota Sorority

Lambda Pi Upsilon

La Raza Law Students Association

Latino Law Students' Association

National Hispanic Business Association

Phi Iota Alpha

Sigma Iota Alpha

Sigma Lambda Gamma

Society for the Advancement of Chicanos and Native Americans in Science

Asian-American

Alpha Kappa Delta Phi

Asian American Student Association

Chi Sigma Phi Sorority

National Association of Asian American Professionals

Nu Alpha Phi fraternity

Pi Delta Psi

Sigma Omicron Pi

Native American

Alaska Native Student Association (ANSA)

Alpha Pi Omega

American Indian Science and Engineering Society

Association of Native American Medical Students

Indian University Scholars Society

Native American Law Student Association

List of Diverse Professional Organizations

Multicultural

National Association of Investment Companies

Minority Corporate Counsel Association

National Association of Minorities in Communications

The Marathon Club

National Organization of Minority Architects

African-American

BUSINESS

Executive Leadership Council

African American MBA Association

American Association of Black Women Entrepreneurs

National Association of Negro Business and Professional
Women's Clubs

National Black MBA Association

Professional Women of Color

LAW AND POLITICS

Blacks in Government

National Association of Black Women Attorneys

National Bar Association

National Organization of Black Law Enforcement Executives

FINANCE AND ACCOUNTING
National Association of Black Accountants

MARKETING, SALES AND ADVERTISING
National Black Public Relations Society

MEDIA AND ENTERTAINMENT
Black Broadcasters Alliance
Organization of Black Screenwriters Inc.

HEALTH CARE
Association of Black Cardiovascular and Thoracic Surgeons
National Black Nurses Association

SCIENCE AND TECHNOLOGY
African American Men in Technology
National Association of Black Telecommunications Professionals Inc.
National Organization for the Advancement of Black Chemists and Chemical Engineers

EDUCATION
Association of African Women Scholars
National Association of African American Studies & Affiliates

OTHER
Black Culinarian Alliance
Coalition of Black Trade Unionists
Organization of Black Airline Pilots

Latino

BUSINESS

Hispanic Association on Corporate Responsibility

National Society of Hispanic MBAs

LAW AND POLITICS

Hispanic National Bar Association

National Association of Latino Elected & Appointed Officials (NALEO)

FINANCE AND ACCOUNTING

Association of Hispanic CPAs

Association of Latino Professionals in Finance and Accounting

MARKETING, SALES, AND ADVERTISING

Association of Hispanic Advertising Agencies

MEDIA AND ENTERTAINMENT

National Association of Hispanic Journalists

HEALTH CARE

National Association of Hispanic Nurses

National Hispanic Medical Association

SCIENCE AND TECHNOLOGY

Professional Hispanics in Energy

Society of Hispanic Professional Engineers

OTHER

National Association of Hispanic Federal Executives

National Hispanic Employee Association (NHEA)

Asian-American

BUSINESS

Asian Women in Business

U.S. Pan Asian American Chamber of Commerce

LAW

National Asian Pacific American Bar Association

MARKETING, SALES, AND ADVERTISING

Asian American Advertising Federation

MEDIA AND ENTERTAINMENT

Asian American Journalists Association

South Asian Journalists Association

Native American

BUSINESS

National Center for American Indian Enterprise Development

National Indian Business Association

CULTURE

Native American Heritage Association

ENVIRONMENT

Alliance of Tribal Tourism Advocates

National Environmental Coalition of Native Americans

LAW AND POLITICS

Alliance for Native American Indian Rights

Northwest Indian Bar Association (NIBA)

FINANCE AND ACCOUNTING

National FSA American Indian Credit Outreach Initiative

HEALTH CARE

Association of American Indian Physicians

National Indian Health Board

MEDIA AND ENTERTAINMENT

Native American Journalists Association

Networking Events

www.multicultural.com. The Web site of Multicultural Marketing Resources Inc. Includes a nationwide calendar of multicultural networking events.

Business

National Association for African Americans in HR National Conference

Training Conference & Inter-Collegiate Jobs Fair

Law

National Asian Pacific American Bar Association Annual Convention

Finance and Accounting

Association of Latino Professionals in Finance and Accounting Convention

National Association of Black Accountants Annual Conference

National Bankers Association Annual Conference

Marketing, Advertising, and Sales

Association of Hispanic Advertising Agencies Semi-Annual Conference

Media and Entertainment

National Association of Hispanic Journalists Annual Convention

National Black Public Relations Society Annual National Conference and Career Fair

South Asian Journalists Association Annual Conference

Health Care

Hispanic Dental Association Annual Meeting

Science and Technology

American Indian Science and Engineering Society National Conference

Black Data Processing Associates Annual National Conference

Chinese Software Professionals Association Annual Conference

Mexican American Engineering Society Annual International Symposium

National Society of Black Engineers Annual Conference

Society of Hispanic Professional Engineers Annual National Technical & Career Conference

Society of Women Engineers National Conference

Miscellaneous

NAACP Diversity Career Fair

National Association of Asian American Professionals Annual Conference

National Urban League Annual Conference

RECRUITING FROM OTHER COMPANIES

Helpful Resources

DiversityInc.com's "Top 50 Companies for Diversity" rankings include:

- top fifty companies for diversity
- top companies for African-Americans
- top companies for Asian-Americans
- top ten companies for Latinos
- top ten companies for recruitment and retention
- top ten companies for supplier diversity

Research online at www.DiversityInc.com.

Fortune provides an annual ranking of the

- fifty best companies for minorities
- top ten employers for African-Americans
- top ten employers for Hispanics
- top ten employers for Asian-Americans
- top ten employers for Native Americans
- companies with largest number of diverse employees among the fifty highest paid
- companies with greatest board diversity
- companies with highest percentage of diverse employees

FINDING CANDIDATES IN
PUBLICATIONS AND ONLINE

Books

Recruiting on the Web: Smart Strategies for Finding the Perfect Candidate. Michael Foster. McGraw-Hill, 2002. A practical guide to finding talent on the Internet, including a small section on diversity.

Job Sites

General Diversity

www.BestDiversityEmployers.com
www.CorpDiversitySearch.com
www.Diversity.com
www.DiversityJobMarket.com
www.DiversityJobNetwork.com
www.DiversityLink.com
www.DiversityWorking.com
www.HireDiversity.com
www.MinorityExecSearch.com

African-American

www.BlackGreekNetwork.com/jobs/
www.BlackVoices.com
www.HBCUCareerCenter.com
www.TBWCareers.com

Latino

www.iHispano.com
www.JobCentro.com
www.LatPro.com

Asian-American

www.Asia-Links.com / asia-jobs
www.Asia-net.com
www.GoldSea.com

8

BUILD YOUR BENCH

You are now well on your way to success in diversity recruiting. You have put your house in order, you have mastered multicultural networking, and you have learned where and how to find the best diversity talent. I have just one more secret to pass along to you: Stop being reactive. Stop recruiting only when a job opens up, and start recruiting every day of every month of every year. As I've said many times in this book, successful recruiting is as much about building relationships as it is about filling a job—and reactive recruiting doesn't leave much time for the relationship part.

See if this story sounds familiar: A hiring manager in your organization needs a positioned filled yesterday, and she'd like to choose from a diverse pool of candidates. As the recruiters begin to diligently research and network, the hiring manager proceeds to pepper them with notes about the importance of the hire. Tensions mount, the notes start getting more pointed, and the recruiters start to cut their losses. Yes, it certainly would be nice to have a diverse pool, but there isn't enough time, and it is a much greater priority to fill the position than to fill the position with a diverse candidate.

This vignette occurs over and over in organizations across America, usually with the same result: lots of white people being hired, and considerable regret year after year about not hiring more equally qualified diverse professionals. Well, this year things are going to be different for your organization. This year, you are going to be prepared because you are going to build a bench of diversity talent long before a job even opens.

I am going to use a baseball analogy here to convey the power of this approach. (Some of you might think this analogy is misplaced, but you'll have to bear with me because I think this is a good one!) You're the coach, it's the bottom of the ninth, the game is tied, and your pitcher is losing steam. You've got to put in a replacement. Fast. You look down the bench. You'd love to put in a left-handed pitcher—but the only one on the team has his arm in a cast. Or worse, he is just up from the minor leagues and normally plays first base. Now the umpire is getting agitated, and the team is getting tense. Then the phone rings—it's the owner calling from the skybox telling you to put in a lefty. But you can't. You failed to plan for this. The umpire yells, "Play ball," you put in a righty, and your team loses.

Too often, this is the predicament in diversity hiring. When the time comes to fill a position, your bench does not have the right players, and there is no time for scouting. It takes thought, planning, and foresight to build the right kind of bench. As you research and network with diverse candidates, you will come across many people who would make wonderful additions to your company. Capture that data and start a list—even if your organization doesn't have open positions for those candidates. If you are a smaller organization, you may want to start a list with twenty-five people. If you are a larger organization, you may want to start several lists of fifty people broken out by department and skill set. Regardless of the number and complexity, your lists should methodically rank and rerank the candidates. A well-managed bench is a living, evolving thing. You should always be refining your list, adding some names and removing others. Be sure to keep the folks who are bumped off your list in your network, however. You may change the frequency and type of interaction with these candidates, but never let them leave your network!

The New York Times Company partners with a variety of professional organizations, including the National Association of Black Journalists and the National Society of Hispanic MBAs, to recruit diverse candidates. The company has mentoring, succession-planning, and career development and training programs in place that will help to avoid this predicament. In 2004, women made up 37 percent of the pool of employees in the succession-planning program. The company's diversity statement includes the goal of "ensuring that the company's executive-succession planning program engages senior management in identifying candidates to rise to certain key positions. Potential leaders are identified and their managers work to provide career-development tools and op-

portunities to the future leaders of the Times Company."
Qualified candidates are reviewed every quarter. (This is an
article/advertising feature by Jason Forsythe. http://www
.nytimes.com/marketing/jobmarket/diversity/development
.html.)

Once you have a list, your goal is to build excellent relationships with the identified candidates. You may not have a job to
offer them, and they may be very happy where they are currently working, but get to know them anyway. Track their careers. Make them feel like you have taken a vested interest in
their future. Even if they never come to work for you, you will
have the benefit of their networks, and a deeper understanding
of the type of candidate you are trying to recruit. For example,
PricewaterhouseCoopers has been an INROADS corporate
sponsor for more than twenty years, and it hosts more than two
hundred interns annually. INROADS is one of a number of organizations that provide an alumni association for their participants, so once the students complete their internships, they
continue to stay in touch with one another and with
PricewaterhouseCoopers. The host company can take advantage of these established relationships and reconnect with former interns or be introduced to new potential hires.

Your bench will likely have several classifications of people:
those who would love to come to work for you right now, those
who might come later under the right conditions, and those
who would probably never work for you but have a huge, diverse network to offer. For those candidates who are not looking for work right away, the bench strategy allows you to
position yourself for the future. It might be six months or six
years before a particular candidate decides to move—but in the
meantime, you are giving that person a favorable impression of

your organization, hopefully one that he or she will share with friends and associates. In essence, you are creating PR agents throughout various communities of color.

Building these relationships does not need to be a herculean effort, but it does need to be consistent. A great first step for entry-level candidates would be to introduce your company and send along copies of your monthly newsletter. For more senior candidates, you could arrange informal dinners with members of your executive team. The messaging and networking steps to take here are very much the same as those we've discussed in previous chapters. Most important, plan out your approach and be consistent over time.

Building a bench not only will improve the odds that your company will hire more diversity candidates, it can also flush out any hidden biases and agendas within your organization. Building a robust pool of candidates shines a bright light on both process and behavior. Once there are strong numbers of qualified diverse candidates moving through your system, if your numbers still don't move, you'll know you have a different kind of problem. Identifying and addressing such problems will enable you to meet your hiring goals and head off any budding liabilities.

Take a few minutes now to work through this Action Plan for building a successful diversity recruiting bench.

Build Your Bench

1.   A talent bench puts you in a strong position to get the right people in the right jobs efficiently. Decide how wide and deep your talent bench will be. Do you need a bench for each department? Each set of skills? Each region? How many people ideally will be on the bench at any given time? Set reasonable, manageable, and achievable metrics.

_____

_____

_____

_____

_____

2.   In diversity recruiting, as in all recruiting, it is efficient to separate candidates into four categories: your "hire right now" candidates, your "they are wonderful but there is no fit at the moment" candidates, your "there is no fit, but they would make a wonderful networking contact" candidates, and your "not now, not ever" candidates. Communicate these categories to the folks who do your networking, and ask them to fit each candidate into one of these categories. Write down your thoughts on how best to begin this process.

_____

_____

_____

_____

3.   Develop your internal plan for communicating with "right now" candidates. Who will meet with them? How will they be most effectively recruited?

_____
_____
_____
_____
_____
_____

4.   Develop your external plan for handling "right now" candidates. How will you set expectations? How will you communicate next steps to the candidates?

_____
_____
_____
_____
_____
_____

5.   Develop your internal plan for handling "maybe later" candidates. Who will be responsible for tracking these candidates and building relationships with them? How will you determine what the next steps are?

_____
_____
_____
_____
_____
_____

6. Develop your external plan for handling "maybe later" candidates. Who will communicate with them? How often? In what format? How will you communicate the next steps to them?

_____

_____

_____

_____

_____

_____

7. Develop your internal plan for handling "no fit, but great for networking" candidates. Who will maintain these relationships?

_____

_____

_____

_____

_____

_____

8. Develop your external plan for handling "no fit, but great for networking" candidates. What will you communicate to these candidates? How? How will you build a lasting, meaningful relationship with them?

_____

_____

_____

_____

_____

RECOMMENDED RESOURCES

Build Your Bench

"Man with a (Talent) Plan." Anna Muoio. *FastCompany Magazine,* January 2001. Discusses the successful bench-building strategy used by Electronic Arts Inc.

9

MEASURE YOUR SUCCESS

You are now well on your way to having more diversity candidates. But how will you know when you have done enough? Without a measurable, achievable goal, the most inspired of initiatives can die. What gets measured gets done—so by shrugging off the issue of measurement, diversity becomes like a greased pig. Everyone chases it, but no one ever gets his hands on it. If you let this happen, you will seriously compromise the success of your initiative.

There is no single, perfect way to measure diversity, but that has never stopped organizations from measuring a whole host of other initiatives. For the last time in this book, I will point you back to the idea of suspended business logic. We all know there are a million ways to slice and dice any piece of data. Someone just needs to make the call. Recruiting presents any number of obvious metrics—everything from telephone calls made, to interviews conducted, to offers extended and accepted. This is another one of those topics about which entire books could be written—and have been. I've recommended a couple at the end of this chapter. Yes, this is more homework, but it's important for you to dig into this issue and match the right metrics to the right goals for your particular organization. Kraft measures the representation of women in middle management and uses this data to project (and increase) the number of women in senior management. The company also looks at percentages of people of color in middle- and senior-management positions as part of its efforts to increase these numbers across the board. It established metrics, monitors the progress, measures the outcomes, and makes the appropriate adjustments.

Regardless of the measure you choose, set a goal that your organization can drive toward. It is hard to hold people accountable when you can't set a benchmark, and there is no faster way to create chaos and inefficiency than to turn your people loose on a project for which there is no finish line. This issue of accountability may make you uncomfortable—and it should. At the end of the day, either you are committed to diversity or you aren't. The numbers will surely tell the story.

The following Action Plan will help you get started outlining the best way to measure the success of your diversity initiative.

A C T I O N   P L A N

Measure Your Success

1. How is your organization measuring your diversity initiative today? Who is setting the metrics, and why? Is this method of measurement working? If you don't have a method of measurement, why not?

_____

_____

_____

_____

_____

2. Much has been written about how to measure and benchmark your company's diversity initiatives. Find a great book on the topic and read it; write your observations here.

_____

_____

_____

_____

_____

3. Make a list of the methods of measurement that would work best for your company, and evaluate the pros and cons of each.

_____

_____

_____

_____

4. How will these methods be implemented? What ob-
stacles will you have to overcome internally? Whose
buy-in will you need to obtain? Begin working on an
implementation plan.

_____

_____

_____

_____

_____

_____

5. Be sure to communicate your achievements
effectively—both internally and externally. Revisit
your communication strategy to ensure ongoing communication of achievements.

_____

_____

_____

_____

_____

_____

RECOMMENDED RESOURCES

Measure Your Success

BOOKS

Action Books: Diversity Breakthrough! Strategic Action Series. Debbe
Kennedy et al. Berrett-Koehler, 2000. A series of six booklets.

The fifth in the series, *Achievement,* helps you create a plan for measuring and celebrating success.

The Diversity Scorecard. Edward E. Hubbard. Butterworth-Heinemann, 2003. A practical book written by one of the leaders in the diversity measurement field, this book provides the strategic and tactical information your organization needs to develop appropriate and effective diversity metrics.

CONCLUSION

For years now, I've been successful at finding and recruiting talented people of color. I've done this for Fortune 500 companies, start-ups, state governments, and nonprofits. And now, in this book, at the risk of putting myself out of business, I've told you everything I know. But I'm not too worried about losing business; let me tell you why. For every one of you who takes this book to heart and really gets busy, there are three or four of you who will get high on the promise of this book, but do nothing of any consequence.

Even more dangerous than those who say they will, but

won't, or don't, are those who proceed in a potentially devastating way. I have seen several clients embark on a search for perfection. These organizations seek the "super minorities" who would be perfect for the organization. Several of my clients have gone so far as to suggest they are looking for a "Jackie Robinson" to come into their business. These types of expectations are incredibly dangerous and have the potential to cause significant harm to your diversification efforts. Even more important, these misplaced expectations place an unfair and unachievable burden on your minority employees. I implore you to resist this type of thinking at all costs. There is simply no substitute for credible, sustained leadership focused on diversity.

As I said in the introduction, fear and complacency are powerful things. Your comfort zone will never stop calling you. You may do a few things here and there to improve your diversity recruiting, but you won't actually force yourself out into new networks until the powerful reality of our multicultural tomorrow whacks you in the face—and by then it will be too late.

I'm not trying to scare you. I'm just trying to help you see around a corner. By doing nothing, you are actually doing something, and the long-term consequences for your organization will not be good. If you take the actions outlined in this book—strip away your excuses, get your house in order, refine your messaging, master multicultural networking, find diversity candidates, build your bench, and measure your success— you will be leaps and bounds ahead of the competition. It's your choice. Will you be one of the few winners, or one of the many losers?

Regardless of what you do, or what you take away from this book, please at least be honest about what is really going on in your organization, and call your lack of diversity what it is: say "This is not a high enough priority for us to commit the resources," or "We don't see the link between diversity and our success," or "I've tried but the organization doesn't support it." Something—anything—other than "We can't find any." You can find diverse candidates. You know you can. This book makes sure you can. You can choose to do it or choose not to do it; but you can no longer say that it *can't* be done.

APPENDICES

Appendix A: Recommended Books

Appendix B: Recommended Web Sites

Appendix C: Top Companies for Diversity

Appendix D: Historically Black or Predominantly African-American Colleges and Universities

Appendix E: Top Degree-Granting Institutions—All Minorities

Appendix F: Top Degree-Granting Institutions—Hispanics

Appendix G: Top Degree-Granting Institutions—Asian-Americans

Appendix H: Top Degree-Granting Institutions—African-Americans

Appendix I: Top Diverse Professional Organizations

Appendix J: Top Diversity Recruiting Web Sites

Appendix K: Diverse Student Organizations

Appendix L: Diverse Media Options

APPENDIX A:
RECOMMENDED BOOKS

Action Books: Diversity Breakthrough! Debbe Kennedy et. al. Berrett-Koehler, 2000.

The Business Case for Diversity. DiversityInc, 2003.

Coaching and Mentoring for Dummies. Marty Brounstein. For Dummies, 2000.

Corporate Performance Management: How to Build a Better Organization Through Measurement-Driven, Strategic Alignment. David Wade and Ron Recardo. Butterworth-Heinemann, 2001.

Creating the Multicultural Organization: A Strategy for Capturing the Power of Diversity. Taylor Cox. Jossey-Bass, 2001.

Diversity and the Bottom Line: Prospering in the Global Economy. Pamela K. Henry. TurnKey Press, 2003.

Diversity Blues: How To Shake 'Em. Gladys Gossett Hankins. Telvic Press, 2000.

Diversity in Organizations. Myrtle P. Bell. South-Western College Publishers, 2006.

The Diversity Recruitment Advertising Toolkit. Tracey De Morsella, ed. Convergence Media, 2006.

The Diversity Scorecard. Edward E. Hubbard. Butterworth-Heinemann, 2003.

The Diversity Training Handbook: A Practical Guide to Understanding and Changing Attitudes. 2nd ed. Phil Clements and John Jones. Kogan Page, 2006.

Do You See What I See: A Diversity Tale for Retaining People of Color. Janice Fenn and Chandra Goforth Irvin. Pfeiffer, 2005.

The Elements of Mentoring. W. Brad Johnson and Charles R. Ridley. Palgrave Macmillian, 2004.

The Employers' Legal Handbook. 7th ed. Fred Steingold and Amy Delpo. Nolo Press, 2005.

Harvard Business Review on Finding and Keeping the Best People. Peter Cappelli and Ibarra Hermina. Harvard Business School Press, 2001.

Harvard Business Review on Managing Diversity. R. Roosevelt Thomas, David A. Thomas, Robin J. Ely, and Debra Meyerson. Harvard Business School Press, 2002.

Impact of Diversity Initiatives on the Bottom Line. Society for Human Resource Management. Society for Human Resource Management, 2002.

The Inclusion Breakthrough. Frederick A. Miller and Judy H. Katz. Berrett-Koehler, 2002.

Keeping the People Who Keep You in Business: 24 Ways to Hang On to Your Most Valuable Talent. F. Leigh Branham. American Management Association, 2000.

The Knowing-Doing Gap: How Smart Companies Turn Knowledge into Action. Jeffrey Pfeffer and Robert I. Sutton. Harvard Business School Press, 2000.

Making Diversity Work: Seven Steps for Defeating Bias in the Workplace. Sondra Thiederman. Kaplan Business, 2003.

The Manager's Pocket Guide to Diversity Management. Edward Hubbard. HRD Press, 2003.

Managing Cultural Diversity in Technical Professions. Lionel Laroche. Butterworth-Heinemann, 2002.

Managing People Across Cultures. Fons Trompenaars and Charles Hampden-Turner. Capstone, 2004.

Masters of Networking. Ivan R. Misner and Don Morgan. Bard Press, 2000.

Measuring Performance: Using the New Metrics to Deploy Strategy and Improve Performance. 2nd ed. Bob Frost. Measurement International, 2000.

Mentoring and Diversity. David Clutterback and Belle Rose Ragins. Butterworth-Heinemann, 2001.

Power Networking: 59 Secrets for Personal and Professional Success. 2nd ed. Donna Fisher. Bard Press, 2000.

Putting Diversity to Work: How to Successfully Lead a Diverse Workforce (50-Minute Book). Simma Lieberman, George Simons, and Kate Berardo. Crisp Learning, 2003.

Reversing the Ostrich Approach to Diversity: Pulling Your Head out of the Sand. A. S. Tolbert. Nasus, 2002.

The 7 Hidden Reasons Employees Leave: How to Recognize the Subtle Signs and Act Before It's Too Late. Leigh Branham. American Management Association, 2005.

7 Keys 2 Success: Unlocking the Passion for Diversity. Rosalyn Taylor O'Neale. Llumina Press, 2005.

The 10 Lenses: Your Guide to Living and Working in a Multicultural World. Mark A. Williams. Capital Books, 2001.

Topgrading: How Leading Companies Win by Hiring, Coaching, and Keeping the Best People. Bradford D. Smart. Portfolio, 2005.

Working Together: Producing Synergy by Honoring Diversity. Mikhail Gorbachev and Angeles Arrien, eds. Berrett-Koehler, 2001.

APPENDIX B:
RECOMMENDED WEB SITES

GENERAL—MULTICULTURAL

www.WithoutExcuses.com

www.ELCINFO.com

www.DiverseEducation.com

www.CensusScope.com

www.NMCI.org—National Multi-Cultural Institute

www.CareerJournal.com

www.DiversityBestPractices.com

www.DiversityWeb.com

www.DiversityCentral.com

www.DiversityBusiness.com

www.SHRM.org/Diversity

www.AIMD.org—American Institute for Managing Diversity

www.DiversityWorking.com

www.NAMIC.org—National Association of Minorities in Communications

www.DiversityatWork.com

www.ICIC.org—Initiative for Competitive Inner Cities

www.TheMarathonClub.org

www.NAICVC.com—National Association of Investment Companies

AFRICAN-AMERICAN

www.DiverseEducation.com
www.BlackVoices.com
www.BlackAmericaWeb.com
www.Black-Collegian.com
www.Inroads.org
www.NUL.org—National Urban League
www.BCW.org—Black Career Women
www.HBCUConnect.com
www.NSBE.org—National Society of Black Engineers
www.BlackEnterprise.com
www.NABJ.com—National Association of Black Journalist
www.NAACP.org

HISPANIC

www.PewHispanic.org—Pew Trusts Hispanic Center
www.NCLR.org—National Council of La Raza
www.HispanicFund.org
www.HACU.org—Hispanic Association of Colleges and Universities
www.LatinoLink.com
www.HispanicOnline.com
www.HispanicBusiness.com
www.SHPE.org—Society of Hispanic Professional Engineers

ASIAN-AMERICAN

www.AAFE.org—Asian Americans for Equality
www.AsiaMedia.com
www.GoldSea.com
www.GoldSea.com/profiles/100—top 100 Asian business owners in United States

NATIVE AMERICAN

www.Indians.org—American Indian Heritage Foundation
www.epa.gov/indian/map.htm—federally recognized tribes
www.NativeWeb.org

www.NativeCultureLinks.com
www.Indianz.com
www.RedEarth.com
www.UnitedNativeAmerica.org

APPENDIX C:
TOP COMPANIES FOR DIVERSITY

These companies were named according to the criteria set forth by the issuing bodies noted. We provide them as examples of those who have been carefully selected by excellent sources. Their selection was a result of their full participation in the respective submittal processes.

These companies should be looked to for guidance relative to their diversity efforts. I encourage you to review their Web sites as appropriate for best practices.

THIRTY BEST COMPANIES FOR DIVERSITY—
BLACK ENTERPRISE, 2005
AFLAC
American Express Company
ARAMARK
Bank of America
BellSouth Corporation
Citigroup
Coors Brewing Company
DaimlerChrysler Corporation
Darden Restaurants
Eastman Kodak Company
Fannie Mae
Federal Express
General Motors Corporation

IBM Corporation
Marriott International
McDonald's Corporation
MGM MIRAGE
Nordstrom
Pepco Holdings
Pepsi Bottling Group
PepsiCo
PG&E Corporation
Pitney Bowes
Procter & Gamble
Starwood Hotels & Resorts Worldwide
Coca-Cola Company
Verizon Communications
Wal-Mart Stores
Xerox Corporation
Yum! Brands

DIVERSITY INC. TOP FIFTY LIST FOR 2005

Altria Group
Turner Broadcasting System
Citigroup
PepsiCo
Abbott Laboratories
Coca-Cola Company
Xerox
Allstate Insurance Company
Verizon Communications
Kraft Foods
Ford Motor Company
Marriott International
KeyBank
Pepsi Bottling Group
SBC Communications
Sears, Roebuck & Company
Health Care Service Corporation

Tribune Company
Pitney Bowes
HSBC Bank USA
New York Life
American Express Company
General Mills
Merck & Company
JPMorgan Chase
Bank of America
Procter & Gamble
Knight Ridder
Wal-Mart
IKON Office Solutions
Wachovia
Prudential Financial
Bausch & Lomb
Comerica Bank
Unilever Foods N.A.
MetLife
Sprint Corporation
SunTrusts Banks
Colgate-Palmolive
Wells Fargo
Staples
BellSouth
Visteon Corporation
Eastman Kodak Company
Cingular Wireless
Nielsen Media
The Chubb Corporation
General Motors
MasterCard
SC Johnson

APPENDIX D:
HISTORICALLY BLACK OR
PREDOMINANTLY AFRICAN-AMERICAN
COLLEGES AND UNIVERSITIES

Alabama A&M University, Alabama
Alabama State University, Alabama
Albany State College, Georgia
Alcorn State University, Mississippi
Allen University, South Carolina
American Baptist College, Arkansas
University of Arkansas at Pine Bluff, Arkansas
Atlanta Metropolitan College, Georgia
Barber-Scotia College, North Carolina
Benedict College, South Carolina
Bennett College, North Carolina
Berean Institute, Pennsylvania
Bethune-Cookman College, Florida
Bishop State Junior College, Alabama
Bluefield State College, West Virginia
Bowie State University, Maryland
Borough of Manhattan Community College, New York
Central State University, Ohio
Charles R. Drew University of Medicine and Sciences, California
Cheyney University of Pennsylvania, Pennsylvania
Chicago State University, Illinois

Clafin College, South Carolina
Clark Atlanta University, Georgia
Clinton Junior College, South Carolina
Community College of Baltimore, Maryland
Compton Community College, California
Concordia College, Alabama
Coppin State College, Maryland
Cuyahoga Community College, Ohio
Delaware State College, Delaware
Denmark Technical College, South Carolina
Detroit College of Business, Michigan
Dillard University, Louisiana
University of the District of Columbia, Washington, D.C.
Draughons Junior College, Tennessee
East-West University, Illinois
Edward Waters College, Florida
Elizabeth State University, North Carolina
Fayetteville State University, North Carolina
Fisk University, Tennessee
Florida A&M, Florida
Florida Memorial College, Florida
Fort Valley State College, Georgia
Grambling State University, Louisiana
Hampton University, Virginia
Hardbarger Junior College of Business, North Carolina
Harold Washington College, Illinois
Harris-Stowe State College, Missouri
Harry S. Truman College, Illinois
Highland Park Community College, Missouri
Hinds Community College, Mississippi
Howard University, Washington, D.C.
Huston-Tillotson College, Texas
Interboro Institute, New York
Jackson State University, Mississippi
Jarvis Christian College, Texas
J. F. Drake Technical College, Alabama

Johnson C. Smith, North Carolina
Kennedy-King College, Illinois
Kentucky State University, Kentucky
Knoxville College, Tennessee
LaGuardia Community College, New York
Lane College, Tennessee
Langston University, Oklahoma
Lawson State Community College, Alabama
Lewis College of Business, Michigan
Lemoyne-Owen College, Tennessee
Lincoln University, Missouri
Lincoln University, Pennsylvania
Livingstone College, North Carolina
Los Angeles Southwest College, California
Malcolm X College, Illinois
Mary Holmes College, Mississippi
University of Maryland at Eastern Shore, Maryland
Meadows College of Business, Georgia
Medgar Evers College (CUNY), New York
Meharry Medical College, Tennessee
Miles College, Alabama
Mississippi Industrial College, Mississippi
Mississippi Valley State University, Mississippi
Morehouse College, Georgia
Morehouse School of Medicine, Georgia
Morgan State University, Maryland
Morris Brown College, Georgia
Morris College, South Carolina
Natchez Junior College, Mississippi
New York City Technical College, New York
Norfolk State University, Virginia
North Carolina AT&T, North Carolina
North Carolina Central University, North Carolina
Oakwood College, Alabama
Olive Harvey College, Illinois

Paine College, Georgia
Paul D. Camp Community College, Virginia
Paul Quinn College, Texas
Philander Smith College, Arkansas
Phillips Junior College of Charlotte, North Carolina
Phillips Junior College of Columbia, South Carolina
Phillips Junior College of Fayetteville, North Carolina
Phillips Junior College of Memphis, Tennessee
Prairie View A&M University, Texas
Prentiss Normal and Industrial Institute, Mississippi
Roxbury Community College, Massachusetts
Rust College, Mississippi
Saint Augustine's College, North Carolina
Saint Paul's College, Virginia
Savannah State College, Georgia
Sawyer College of Business, Ohio
Shaw College at Detroit, Michigan
Shaw University, North Carolina
Shorter College, Arkansas
Simmons University Bible College, Kentucky
South Carolina State University, South Carolina
Southern University, Louisiana
Spelman College, Georgia
Stillman College, Alabama
Talladega College, Alabama
Trenholm State Technical College, Alabama
Tennessee State University, Tennessee
Texas College, Texas
Tougaloo College, Mississippi
Tuskegee University, Alabama
Virginia Seminary and College, Virginia
Virginia State University, Virginia
Virginia Union University, Virginia
University of the Virgin Islands, U.S. Virgin Islands
Voorhees College, South Carolina

Wayne County Community College, Michigan
Wilberforce University, Ohio
Wiley College, Texas
Winston-Salem University, North Carolina
Xavier University, Louisiana

APPENDIX E:
TOP DEGREE-GRANTING
INSTITUTIONS—ALL MINORITIES

Listed by: all minority groups, African-American, Hispanic, and Asian-American.

All listings are in order by the total number of annual baccalaureate degrees granted according to the ethnic category identified.

University of California–Los Angeles, California
University of California–Berkeley, California
Florida International University, Florida
University of California–Irvine, California
University of Texas at Austin, Texas
California State University–Fullerton, California
University of California–Davis, California
California State University–Long Beach, California
University of Houston–University Park, Texas
University of Florida, Florida
San Francisco State University, California
San Diego State University, California
California State University–Northridge, California
San Jose State University, California
University of Washington–Seattle, Washington
University of Hawaii at Manoa, Hawaii
Rutgers University, New Jersey

University of California–Riverside, California
University of California–San Diego, California
University of Southern California, California
University of Maryland–College Park, Maryland
California State Polytechnic University–Pomona, California
University of Illinois–Urbana Champaign, Illinois
University of Texas at San Antonio, Texas
University of Central Florida, Florida
Florida A&M University, Florida
University of Texas at El Paso, Texas
Florida State University, Florida
California State University–Sacramento, California
University of Texas–Pan American, Texas
University of Illinois at Chicago, Illinois
University of Michigan–Ann Arbor, Michigan
University of South Florida, Florida
University of California–Santa Barbara, California
CUNY Bernard Baruch College, New York
Georgia State University, Georgia
Arizona State University, Arizona
Florida Atlantic University, Florida
University of Arizona, Arizona
Temple University, Pennsylvania
California State University–Dominguez Hills, California
California State University–Fresno, California
Howard University, Washington, D.C.
SUNY at Stony Brook, New York
New York University, New York
University of New Mexico, New Mexico
Ohio State University, Ohio
University of Texas at Arlington, Texas
Michigan State University, Michigan
CUNY Hunter College, New York
California State University–San Bernardino, California
California State University–Hayward, California
Texas A&M University, Texas

Texas State University–San Marcos, Texas
Pennsylvania State University, Pennsylvania
New Mexico State University, New Mexico
Devry University, California
University of North Texas, Texas
California Polytechnic State University–San Luis Obispo, California
University of Maryland–University College, Maryland
Cornell University, New York
Southern University and A&M College, Louisiana
George Mason University, Virginia
University of Miami, Florida
University of California–Santa Cruz, California
St. John's University, New York
University of Houston–Downtown, Texas
CUNY Lehman College, New York
Park University, Missouri
CUNY City College, New York
CUNY John Jay College of Criminal Justice, New York
Mercy College, New York
Strayer University, Washington, D.C.
Tennessee State University, Tennessee
University of Pennsylvania, Pennsylvania
North Carolina AT&T State University, North Carolina
DePaul University, Illinois
Barry University, Florida
University of Nevada–Las Vegas, Nevada
Hampton University, Virginia
Stanford University, California
CUNY Queens College, New York
Jackson State University, Mississippi
Northern Illinois University, Illinois
Morgan State University, Maryland
University of Virginia, Virginia
North Carolina State University at Raleigh, North Carolina
Virginia Commonwealth University, Virginia

Boston University, Massachusetts
University of Minnesota, Minnesota
University of Oklahoma–Norman, Oklahoma
CUNY Brooklyn, New York
SUNY at Buffalo, New York
Kean University, New Jersey
Wayne State University, Michigan
Prairie View A&M University, Texas
Southern Illinois University–Carbondale, Illinois
University of North Carolina at Chapel Hill, North Carolina
Montclair State University, New Jersey
Robert Morris College, Illinois
Devry University–Illinois, Illinois
St. Leo University, Florida

Source: *Black Issues in Higher Education*, 2003–2004
www.diverseeducation.com/Top100home.ASP

APPENDIX F: TOP DEGREE-GRANTING INSTITUTIONS—HISPANICS

Listed by: Hispanic graduates.

All listings are in order by the total number of annual baccalaureate degrees granted according to the ethnic category identified.

Florida International University, Florida
University of Texas–Pan American, Texas
University of Texas at El Paso, Texas
University of Texas at San Antonio, Texas
California State University–Fullerton, California
California State University–Los Angeles, California
California State University–Northridge, California
University of Texas at Austin, Texas
San Diego State University, California
California State University–Long Beach, California
University of Florida, Florida
University of California–Los Angeles, California
New Mexico State University, New Mexico
University of Houston–University Park, Texas
University of Arizona, Arizona
California State University–Fresno, California
Texas State University–San Marcos, Texas

University of Central Florida, Florida
Arizona State University, Arizona
California State University–San Bernardino, California
California State Polytechnic University–Pomona, California
University of California–Santa Barbara, California
University of California–Riverside, California
Texas A&M University, Texas
University of Texas at Brownsville, Texas
California State University–Dominguez Hills, California
University of California–Berkeley, California
University of Miami, Florida
University of Southern California, California
Texas A&M International University, Texas
University of South Florida, Florida
San Jose State University, California
University of California–Davis, California
Florida State University, Florida
University of California–Irvine, California
Florida Atlantic University–Boca Raton, Florida
Barry University, Florida
California State University–Sacramento, California
San Francisco State University, California
Texas A&M University–Kingsville, Texas
University of Illinois at Chicago, Illinois
Devry University–California
CUNY Hunter College, New York
Texas A&M University–Corpus Christi, Texas
Mercy College, New York
CUNY John Jay College of Criminal Justice, New York
University of Texas at Arlington, Texas
University of the Incarnate Word, Texas
California Polytechnic State University–San Luis Obispo, California
CUNY Lehman College, New York
Rutgers University, New Jersey
University of California–Santa Cruz, California
CUNY Bernard M Baruch College, New York

University of California–San Diego, California
Park University, Missouri
Texas Tech University, Texas
University of Houston–Downtown, Texas
Long Island University–CW Post Campus, New York
University of North Texas, Texas
Northern Arizona University, Arizona
St. John's University, New York
University of Illinois at Urbana Champaign, Illinois
St. Mary's University, Texas
California State University–Bakersfield, California
Montclair State University, New Jersey
Kean University, New Jersey
University of Maryland–College Park, Maryland
California State University–Stanislaus, California
CUNY City College, New York
DePaul University, Illinois
University of Phoenix–New Mexico Campus, New Mexico
Pennsylvania State University, Pennsylvania
New Jersey City University, New Jersey
University of Washington–Seattle, Washington
Arizona State University–West, Arizona
California State University–Chico, California
CUNY Queens College, New York
University of Nevada–Las Vegas, Nevada
New York University, New York
Wayland Baptist University, Texas
California State University–Hayward, California
Northeastern Illinois University, Illinois
University of Colorado at Boulder, Colorado
Robert Morris College, Illinois
University of La Verne, California
Our Lady of the Lake University–San Antonio, Texas
University of Phoenix, Southern California, California
University of Michigan–Ann Arbor, Michigan
Loyola Marymount University, California

Devry University–Illinois, Illinois
NOVA Southeastern University, Florida
California State University–San Marcos, California
Metropolitan State College of Denver, Colorado
Sul Ross State University, Texas
Monroe College–Main Campus, Texas
William Paterson University, New Jersey
St. Edwards University, Texas
SUNY at Stony Brook, New York
Colorado State University, Colorado
National University, California

Source: *Black Issues in Higher Education*, 2003–2004
www.diverseeducation.com/Top100home.asp

APPENDIX G:
TOP DEGREE-GRANTING
INSTITUTIONS—ASIAN-AMERICANS

Listed by: Asian-American graduates.

All listings are in order by the total number of annual baccalaureate degrees granted according to the ethnic category identified.

University of California–Berkeley, California
University of California–Los Angeles, California
University of California–Irvine, California
University of Hawaii at Manoa, Hawaii
University of California–Davis, California
University of Washington–Seattle, Washington
University of California–San Diego, California
University of Texas at Austin, Texas
San Francisco State University, California
San Jose State University, California
California State University–Fullerton, California
University of California–Riverside, California
Rutgers University, New Jersey
California State Polytechnic University–Pomona, California
University of Southern California, California
California State University–Long Beach, California
University of Illinois, Urbana Champaign, Illinois

University of Houston–University Park, Texas
University of Maryland–College Park, Maryland
University of Michigan–Ann Arbor, Michigan
San Diego State University, California
University of Illinois at Chicago, Illinois
California State University–Sacramento, California
New York University, New York
SUNY at Stony Brook, New York
University of California–Santa Barbara, California
California State University–Northridge, California
California State University–Hayward, California
CUNY Bernard M. Baruch College, New York
University of Florida, Florida
Cornell University, New York
University of Pennsylvania, Pennsylvania
California State University–Los Angeles, California
California Polytechnic State University–San Luis Obispo,
    California
Ohio State University, Ohio
Stanford University, California
Pennsylvania State University, Pennsylvania
University of California–Santa Cruz, California
Boston University, Massachusetts
Georgia Institute of Technology, Georgia
University of Minnesota, Minnesota
Devry University–California, California
University of Texas at Dallas, Texas
Michigan State University, Michigan
Massachusetts Institute of Technology, Massachusetts
University of Virginia, Virginia
University of Texas–Arlington, Texas
Hawaii Pacific University, Hawaii
SUNY at Buffalo, New York
CUNY Queens College, New York
University of Nevada–Las Vegas, Nevada
Arizona State University–Main Campus, Arizona

Northwestern University, Illinois
University of Central Florida, Florida
University of Arizona, Arizona
California State University–Fresno, California
SUNY at Binghamton, New York
Drexel University, Pennsylvania
University of Maryland–Baltimore County, Maryland
Virginia Polytechnic Institute and State University, Virginia
University of South Florida, Florida
Columbia University, New York
Georgia State University, Georgia
DePaul University, Illinois
CUNY Hunter College, New York
Carnegie Mellon University, Pennsylvania
Pace University, New York
Harvard University, Massachusetts
University of Colorado at Boulder, Colorado
Temple University, Pennsylvania
Portland State University, Oregon
University of Hawaii at Hilo, Hawaii
University of San Francisco, California
New Jersey Institute of Technology, New Jersey
North Carolina State University at Raleigh, North Carolina
St. John's University, New York
Purdue University, Indiana
Texas A&M University, Texas
Northern Illinois University, Illinois
Oregon State University, Oregon
Rutgers University–Newark, New Jersey
University of Wisconsin–Madison, Wisconsin
University of Massachusetts–Amherst, Massachusetts
Emory University, Georgia
University of Connecticut, Connecticut
Santa Clara University, California
Indiana University–Bloomington, Indiana
Brown University, Rhode Island

Tufts University, Massachusetts
University of North Carolina at Chapel Hill, North Carolina
Johns Hopkins University, Maryland
University of Georgia, Georgia
California State University–Dominguez Hills, California
University of Maryland–University College, Maryland
University of Oregon, Oregon
George Washington University, Washington, D.C.
Yale University, Connecticut
Florida State University, Florida
Seattle University, Washington
Virginia Commonwealth University, Virginia
Florida Atlantic University–Boca Raton, Florida

Source: *Black Issues in Higher Education*, 2003–2004
www.diverseeducation.com/Top100home.asp

APPENDIX H:
TOP DEGREE-GRANTING
INSTITUTIONS—AFRICAN-AMERICANS

Listed by: African-American graduates.

All listings are in order by the total number of annual baccalaureate degrees granted according to the ethnic category identified.

Florida A&M, Florida
Howard University, Washington, D.C.
Georgia State University, Georgia
Southern University and A&M College, Louisiana
Temple University, Pennsylvania
Tennessee State University, Tennessee
North Carolina AT&T University, North Carolina
Hampton University, Virginia
Jackson State University, Mississippi
Florida State University, Florida
Morgan State University, Maryland
University of Maryland–College Park, Maryland
Prairie View A&M University, Texas
University of Maryland–University College, Maryland
Norfolk State University, Virginia
Strayer University–Washington Campus, Washington, D.C.
Florida International University, Florida
Chicago State University, Illinois

University of Florida, Florida
Florida Atlantic University–Boca Raton, Florida
North Carolina Central University, North Carolina
University of South Florida, Florida
Michigan State University, Michigan
Alabama State University, Alabama
Grambling State University, Louisiana
University of Houston–University Park, Texas
Georgia Southern University, Georgia
Ohio State University, Ohio
South Carolina State University, South Carolina
Alabama A&M University, Alabama
University of Southern Mississippi, Mississippi
Virginia State University, Virginia
University of Memphis, Tennessee
Spelman College, Georgia
Fayetteville State University, North Carolina
Bowie State University, Maryland
St. Leo University, Florida
University of Central Florida, Florida
University of South Carolina–Columbia, South Carolina
George Mason University, Virginia
Southern Illinois University–Carbondale, Illinois
Wayne State University, Michigan
California State University–Dominguez Hills, California
Virginia Commonwealth University, Virginia
Southern University at New Orleans, Louisiana
CUNY York College, New York
Old Dominion University, Virginia
Mississippi State University, Mississippi
CUNY City College, New York
Albany State University, Georgia
University of North Texas, Texas
CUNY Lehman College, New York
Park University, Missouri
Rutgers University, New Jersey

CUNY Brooklyn College, New York
Xavier University of Louisiana, Louisiana
Morehouse College, Georgia
East Carolina University, North Carolina
Texas Southern University, Texas
College of New Rochelle, New York
Clark-Atlanta University, Georgia
Tuskegee University, Alabama
University of North Carolina at Charlotte, North Carolina
University of North Carolina at Chapel Hill, North Carolina
CUNY Hunter College, New York
Mercy College, New York
CUNY John Jay College of Criminal Justice, New York
CUNY Bernard M. Baruch College, New York
North Carolina State University at Raleigh, North Carolina
University of Alabama, Alabama
Robert Morris College, Illinois
Benedict College, South Carolina
University of Houston–Downtown, Texas
University of Illinois at Urbana Champaign, Illinois
Louisiana State University and A&M, Louisiana
Eastern Michigan University, Michigan
University of Michigan–Ann Arbor, Michigan
Winston-Salem State University, North Carolina
University of Alabama at Birmingham, Alabama
University of North Carolina at Greensboro, North Carolina
University of Texas at Arlington, Texas
Shaw University, North Carolina
Troy State University, Alabama
American Inter-Continental University–Atlanta, Georgia
Pennsylvania State University, Pennsylvania
Dillard University, Louisiana
Delaware State University, Delaware
National-Louis University, Illinois
Northern Illinois University, Illinois
Wayland Baptist University, Texas

University of Louisiana at Lafayette, Louisiana
Monroe College, New York
St. John's University, New York
Alcorn State University, Mississippi
SUNY at Stony Brook, New York
Devry University–Georgia, Georgia
University of New Orleans, Louisiana
University of Arkansas at Pine Bluff, Arkansas
University of Maryland Eastern Shore, Maryland
Middle Tennessee State University, Tennessee

Source: *Black Issues in Higher Education*, 2003–2004
www.diverseeducation.com/Top100home.asp

APPENDIX I:
TOP DIVERSE PROFESSIONAL
ORGANIZATIONS

MULTICULTURAL

National Association of Investment Companies
American Association of Minority Businesses
Conference of Minority Public Administrators
Minority Corporate Counsel Association
Minority Technology Entrepreneurs
The Marathon Club
National Association of Minorities in Communications
National Minority Business Council
National Organization of Minority Architects

AFRICAN-AMERICAN

Business

The Executive Leadership Council
African American MBA Association
African American Women Business Owners Association
African American Women Entrepreneurs at Home
American Association of Black Women Entrepreneurs
American Association of Minority Business
Black Business Professionals and Entrepreneurs
Caribbean-American Chamber of Commerce & Industry
Evening Black Management Association

National Association of Negro Business and Professional Women's Clubs
National Black Business Trade Association
National Black MBA Association
National Business League
National Institute for Women of Color
National Minority Business Council
National Minority Supplier Diversity Council
Professional Black Women's Enterprise
Professional Women of Color

Law and Politics

Blacks in Government
National Association of Blacks in Criminal Justice
National Association of Black Women Attorneys
National Bar Association
National Black Law Students Association
National Black Police Association
National Organization of Black Law Enforcement Executives

Finance and Accounting

National Association of Black Accountants
National Bankers Association
Urban Financial Services Coalition National Association of Urban Bankers

Marketing, Sales, and Advertising

National Black Public Relations Society

Media and Entertainment

Black Broadcasters Alliance
Black Women in Publishing
National Association of Black Journalists
National Association of Black Owned Broadcasters
National Association of Minority Media Executives
National Newspaper Publishers Association (Black Press of America)
Organization of Black Screenwriters Inc.

Health Care

Association for the Advancement of Blacks in Health Sciences
Association of Black Cardiologists
Association of Black Cardiovascular and Thoracic Surgeons
Association of Black Psychologists
Institute for African American Health
National Black Nurses Association
National Black Women's Health Project
National Dental Association
National Medical Association

Science and Technology

African American Men in Technology
African American Women in Technology
Alliance of Black Technical Organizations
American Association of Blacks in Energy
Association of African American Web Developers
Association of Black Sociologists
Black Data Processing Associates
Black Graduate Engineering and Science Students
Blacks in Technology
National Association of Black Telecommunications Professionals Inc.
National Association of Minority Engineering Program Administrators
National Organization for the Professional Development of Black Chemists and Chemical Engineers
National Society of Black Engineers

Education

African Studies Association
Association of African Women Scholars
National Alliance of Black School Educators
National Association of African American Studies & Affiliates
National Association of Colleges and Employers

Other
Black Culinarian Alliance
Coalition of Black Trade Unionists
Conference of Minority Transportation Officials
National Association of Black Social Workers
National Coalition of 100 Black Women
National Forum for Black Public Administrators
Organization of Black Airline Pilots

LATINO

Business
Hispanic Association on Corporate Responsibility
Hispanic Network of Entrepreneurs
Hispanic Organization of Professionals & Executives
Latin Business Association
National Hispanic Business Association
National Network of Hispanic Women
National Society for Hispanic Professionals
National Society of Hispanic MBAs
U.S. Hispanic Chamber of Commerce

Law and Politics
Hispanic National Bar Association
National Association of Latino Elected & Appointed Officials
(NALEO)

Finance and Accounting
Association of Hispanic CPAs
Association of Latino Professionals in Finance and Accounting
National Association of Hispanic Investors & Advisors

Marketing, Sales, and Advertising
Association of Hispanic Advertising Agencies
Hispanic Public Relations Association

Media and Entertainment

National Association of Hispanic Journalists

Health Care

National Alliance for Hispanic Health

National Association of Hispanic Nurses

National Coalition of Hispanic Mental Health & Human Services Organizations

National Hispanic Medical Association

Science and Technology

Professional Hispanics in Energy

Society for Advancement of Chicanos & Native Americans in Science

Society of Hispanic Professional Engineers

Other

National Association of Hispanic Federal Executives

National Community for Latino Leadership

National Hispanic Employee Association (NHEA)

ASIAN

Business

Asian Women in Business

U.S. Pan Asian American Chamber of Commerce

Law

National Asian Pacific American Bar Association

Marketing, Sales, and Advertising

Asian American Advertising Federation

Media and Entertainment

Asian American Journalists Association

South Asian Journalists Association

NATIVE AMERICAN

Business

National Center for American Indian Enterprise Development
National Indian Business Association

Culture

Native American Heritage Association

Environment

Alliance of Tribal Tourism Advocates
Council for Indigenous Arts and Culture
National Aboriginal Forestry Association
National Association of Tribal Historic Preservation Officers
National Environmental Coalition Of Native Americans

Law and Politics

Alliance for Native American Indian Rights
First American Education Project
Minnesota American Indian Bar Association (MAIBA)
National Congress of American Indians
National Indian Justice Center
National Native American Bar Association
National Native American Law Enforcement Association
Navajo Nation Bar Association
Northwest Indian Bar Association (NIBA)

Finance and Accounting

National FSA American Indian Credit Outreach Initiative

Health Care

Association of American Indian Physicians
National Council of Urban Indian Health
National Indian Child Welfare Association (NICWA)
National Indian Health Board

Media and Entertainment

Native American Journalists Association

Science and Technology

Society for the Advancement of Chicanos and Native Americans in Science

Education

First Nations Development Institute
National Indian Youth Leadership Project (NIYLP)

Other

American Indian Library Association

APPENDIX J:
TOP DIVERSITY
RECRUITING WEB SITES

www.AmericanDiversityJobs.com
www.AsiaCareers.com
www.Asia-Links.com/Asia-Jobs
www.AsiaMedia.com
www.Asia-Net.com
www.Asian-Jobs.com
www.BlackEnterprise.com
www.BlackGreekNetwork.com
www.BlackVoices.com
www.CareerPlace.com
www.Diversity.com
www.DiversityBusiness.com
www.DiversityInc.com
www.DiversityLink.com
www.DiversitySearch.com
www.DiversityWorking.com
www.EOP.com
www.Goldsea.com
www.HBCUCareerCenter.com
www.HBCUConnect.com
www.HispanicBusiness.com
www.HispanicCareers.com
www.Hispanic-Jobs.com

www.HispanicOnline.com
www.iHispano.com
www.IMDiversity.com
www.inroads.org
www.JobCentral.com
www.JobCentro.com
www.JournalismJobs.com
www.LatPro.com
www.MinorityExecSearch.com
www.MinorityHire.com
www.NABJ.com
www.NativeAmericanJobs.com
www.NBMBAA.org (National Black MBA Association)
www. ndnjobs.com
www.NSHMBA.com (National Society of Hispanic MBAs)
www.NUL.org (National Urban League)
www.Saludos.com
www.TBWCareers.com
www.Vault.com
www.WomenandMinorities.com
www.WomensJobSearch.net
www.WorkplaceDiversity.com

APPENDIX K:
DIVERSE STUDENT
ORGANIZATIONS

MULTICULTURAL
Cross Cultural Association
Minorities in Public Policy
Minority Graduate Students Association
Multicultural Student Organizations

AFRICAN-AMERICAN
African American MBA Association
Alpha Kappa Alpha Sorority
Alpha Phi Alpha Fraternity
Association of Black Graduates and Professional Students
Black Business Students Association
Black Engineering and Science Students
Black Graduate Engineering and Science Students
Black Law Students' Association
Black Leadership Association
Black Pre-Law Society
Black Pre-Medical Association
Black Student Alliance
Black Students in Health Associations
Concerned Black Men
Delta Sigma Theta Sorority

Gamma Phi Delta Sorority
Groove Phi Groove
Iota Phi Lambda Sorority
Iota Phi Theta Fraternity
Kappa Alpha Psi Fraternity
National Association for the Advancement of Colored People
National Council of Negro Women
National Society of Black Engineers
Omega Psi Phi Fraternity
100 College Black Men
Phi Beta Sigma Fraternity
Sigma Gamma Rho Sorority
Zeta Phi Beta Sorority

LATINO

ALIANZA: The Latina/o Student Alliance
Alpha Psi Lambda
Aspira Association
Chi Upsilon Sigma
College Hispanic American Students
Collegiate Leadership Network
Hermandad de Sigma Iota Sorority
Hispanic Engineers and Scientists
Kappa Delta Chi Sorority
Lambda Pi Upsilon
Lambda Theta Alpha Latin Sorority
Lambda Theta Phi
La Raza Law Students Association
Latin American MBA Association
Latin American Student Organization
Latino Law Students' Association
Latino Students Association
Latino/a Association of Graduate Students in Engineering
and Science
Latinos in Health Organization

National Association of Chicano Studies
National Hispanic Business Association
Omega Delta Phi
Phi Iota Alpha
Sigma Iota Alpha
Sigma Lambda Beta
Sigma Lambda Gamma
Society for the Advancement of Chicanos and Native Americans in Science
Society of Hispanic Professional Engineers

ASIAN

Alpha Kappa Delta Phi
Anime Club
Asian American Exchange
Asian American Journalist Association
Asian American Student Association
Asian Business Association
Asian Political Association
Chi Sigma Phi Sorority
Chinese Student Association
Lambda Phi Epsilon
National Association of Asian American Professionals
Nu Alpha Phi fraternity
Pi Delta Psi
Sigma Beta Rho Fraternity
Sigma Omicron Pi

NATIVE AMERICAN

Alaska Native Student Association (ANSA)
Alpha Pi Omega
American Indian Science and Engineering Society
Association of Native American Medical Students
Beta Sigma Epsilon
Cherokee Student Group
Indian University Scholars Society

Native American Law Student Association
Native American Student Association
Phi Sigma Nu
RezNet News: News & Views by Native American Students

APPENDIX L:
DIVERSE MEDIA OPTIONS

AFRICAN-AMERICAN

Broadcast

TELEVISION
BET—Black Entertainment Television www.bet.com
Top Television Networks Among African-Americans (Based on Nielsen Data)
FOX www.fox.com
UPN www.upn.com
CBS www.cbs.com
ABC www.abc.com

Newspapers in Major Cities (African-American population = 30,000+)

WEST/SOUTHWEST/MIDWEST
African-American News & Issues (Dallas) www.aframnews.com
Chicago Defender www.chicagodefender.com
Chicago Standard standardnewspapers.com
Cincinnati Herald www.cincinnatiherald.com
City News (Cleveland) www.citynewsohio.com
Communicator News (Cincinnati) thecommunicatornews.com
Dallas Post Tribune www.dallaspost.com
Dallas Weekly www.dallasweekly.com
Final Call (Chicago) www.finalcall.com
Insight News (Minnesota) www.insightnews.com

Los Angeles Sentinel www.losangelessentinel.com/index.html
Milwaukee Courier www.milwaukeecourier.org
Milwaukee Times www.milwtimes.com
San Francisco Bay View www.sfbayview.com
Skanner (Portland, Ore.; Seattle) www.theskanner.com
Tri-State Defender Newspaper www.tri-statedefender.com
Windy City Word www.windycityword.com

EAST/NORTHEAST/SOUTHEAST

Amsterdam News (New York) www.amsterdamnews.org
Atlanta Daily World www.atlantadailyworld.com
Atlanta Inquirer theatlantainquirer.net
Atlanta Tribune www.atlantatribune.com
Atlanta Voice www.theatlantavoice.com
Baltimore Times www.btimes.com
Baltimore/Washington, D.C., Afro-American www.afro.com
Baton Rouge Weekly Press www.theweeklypress.com
Bay State Banner www.baystatebanner.com
Birmingham Times thebirminghamtimes.com
Black Chronicle (Oklahoma) www.blackchronicle.com
Black Star News (Texas) www.blackstarnews.com
Capital Outlook (Florida) www.capitaloutlook.com
Carolina Peacemaker (Durham, N.C.) www.carolinapeacemaker
    .com
Charlotte Post www.thecharlottepost.com
Columbus Times (Ga.) www.columbustimes.com
Dallas Examiner www.dallasexaminer.com
Eagle News www.eaglenews.com
Indianapolis Recorder www.indianapolisrecorder.com
Jackson Advocate (Jackson, Miss.) www.jacksonadvocate.com
Mississippi Link www.mississippilink.com
Monroe Free Press www.monroefreepress.com
New Journal & Guide (Hampton, Va.) www.njournalg.com
New Pittsburgh Courier www.newpittsburghcourier.com
New York Beacon newyorkbeacon.com
Newark City News newarkcitynews.com
Orlando Times www.orlandotimes.dsiwebbuilder.com

Philadelphia Sunday Sun www.philasun.com
Philadelphia Tribune www.phila-tribune.com
Tennessee Tribune www.thetennesseetribune.com
Weekly Challenger (Tampa, Fla.) theweeklychallenger.com
Westside Gazette (Miami) www.thewestsidegazette.com

OTHER

African Sun Times www.africansuntimes.com
Black PR Wire www.blackprwire.com
Haiti Progress www.haitiprogres.com
U.S. African Voice www.usafricanvoice.com

Magazines

about . . . time Magazine wwwabouttimemag.com
African Voices www.africanvoices.com
American Legacy www.americanlegacymag.com
Bahiyah Woman Magazine www.bwmmag.com
Black Collegian www.blackcollegian.com
Black Enterprise www.blackenterprise.com
Black E.O.E. Journal www.blackeoejournal.com
Black Family Digest www.familydigest.com
Black Issues Book Review www.bibookreview.com
Diverse: Issues in Higher Education www.diverseeducation.com
Dominican Times Magazine www.dominicantimes.com
Ebony www.ebony.com
Essence www.essence.com
Heart and Soul www.heartandsoul.com
Imani www.imanimag.com
Jet www.jetmag.com
KIP Business Report www.kipbusinessreport.com
Mosaic www.mosaicmagazine.org
Network Journal www.tnj.com
O, the Oprah Magazine www.oprah.com/omagazine
Onyx Woman www.onyxwoman.com
Savoy www.savoymag.com
Sister 2 Sister www.s2smagazine.com
Souls: A Critical Journal www.columbia.edu/cu/ccbh/souls

Upscale Magazine www.upscalemagazine.com
Urban Network www.urbannetwork.com
Urban Spectrum Magazine www.urbanspectrum.net
U.S. Black Engineer Magazine www.blackengineer.com
Vibe www.vibe.com
XXL www.xxlmag.com

HISPANIC

Broadcast

TELEVISION
CNN en Español www.cnnenespanol.com
Entravision Communications www.entravision.com
Hispanic Information Telecommunications Network www.hitn
  .org
KCSO-TV (Sacramento/Stockton/Modesto) www.kcso33.com
KJLA (Los Angeles) www.kjla.com
Más Música Teve www.masmusica.tv
Telefutura www.telefutura.com
Telemundo www.telemundo.com
Tu TV www.tutv.puertorico.pr
Univision www.univision.net

RADIO
A comprehensive list of Hispanic radio stations is available at
www.RDSMarketing.com/NHED.html

Major Print (daily) (circulation 100,000+)
El Diario www.diario.com.mx
El Mexicano www.el-mexicano.com.mx
El Nuevo Dia www.elnuevodia.net
El Nuevo Herald (*The Miami Herald*) www.elnuevoherald.com
El Sentinal www.sun-sentinel.com/elsentinal
El Vocero do Puerto Rico www.vocero.com
La Opinión www.laopinion.com
San Juan Star (Star Media Network) www.thesanjuanstar.com

Magazines

Casa & Estilo Internacional Magazine www.casaestilo.com
Catalina Magazine www.catalinamagazine.com
Estylo Magazine www.estylo.com
Hispanic Journal www.hispanicjournal.com
Hispanic Magazine www.hispanicmagazine.com
Hispanic Network Magazine www.hnmagazine.com
Hispanic Outlook in Higher Education Magazine www.hispanic
outlook.com
Hispanic Today Magazine www.hispanic-today.com
La Salud Hispana Magazine www.lasaludhispana.com
Latin Beat Magazine www.latinbeatmagazine.com
Latin Business Magazine www.latinbusinessmag.com
Latin Style www.latinstylemag.com
Latina Style www.latinastyle.com
Latina www.latina.com
LatinFinance Magazine www.latinfinance.com
Latino Leaders www.latinoleaders.com
Urban Latino www.urbanlatino.com
Vista Magazine www.vistamagazine.com

OTHER
Hispanic PR Wire www.hispanicprwire.com

ASIAN-AMERICAN
Broadcast
TELEVISION
Asia Television (ATV) www.hkatv.com
Asian Television Network www.asiantelevision.com
Television Asia www.tvasia.com.sg

Newspapers
Asian American Press (Minnesota) www.aapress.com
Asian Journal (West Coast) www.asianjournal.com
Asian Pages (Midwest) www.asianpages.com
Asian Week news.asianweek.com
Balita (Filipino) www.balita.com

Filipino Express www.filipinoexpress.com
Filipino Reporter www.filipinoreporter.com
Hokubei Mainichi (Japanese—San Francisco) www.hokubei.com
India Abroad www.indiaabroad.com
India Post www.indiapost.com
Indian Express www.indianexpress.com
IndUS Business Journal www.indusbusinessjournal.com
Korea Central Daily www.joongangusa.com
Nichi Bei Times (Japanese—California) www.nichibeitimes.com
Northwest Asian Weekly www.nwasianweekly.com
Pakistan Link www.pakistanlink.com
Pakistan Today www.paktoday.com
Philippine News www.philnews.com
Sing Tao Newspapers Limited (Chinese—West Coast) www.singtaousa.com
Vietnam Daily News www.vietnamdaily.com

Magazines

Asiance Magazine www.asiancemagazine.com
Biz India www.bizindia.net
Diya www.diyamagazine.com
Filipinas www.filipinasmag.com
Hyphen www.hyphenmagazine.com
Jade Magazine www.jademagazine.com
Kyoto Journal www.kyotojournal.org
Little India www.littleindia.com
Nirvana Woman www.nirvanawoman.net
Philippine Post Magazine www.philpost.com
Rivaaj Magazine www.rivaajmagazine.com
Silicon India www.siliconindia.com

NATIVE AMERICAN

Broadcast

TELEVISION

Aboriginal Peoples Television Network www.aptn.ca
Native American Public Telecommunications www.native
telecom.org
Native American Television Inc. www.natv.org

Newspapers

Aboriginal Multi-Media Society of Alberta www.ammsa.com
Cherokee Observer www.cherokeeobserver.org
Chickasaw Times www.chickasaw.net
Circle www.thecirclenews.org
Indian Country Today www.indiancountry.com
Native American Times www.nativetimes.com
Native Voice www.native-voice.com
Navajo Hopi Observer www.navajohopiobserver.com
Navajo Times www.thenavajotimes.com
Ojibwe Press www.press-on.net
Sho-Ban News www.shobannews.com

Magazines

Cultural Survival www.cs.org
Independent American Indian Review www.worldviewsintl.com/
iair
Native Peoples Magazine www.nativepeoples.com
News from Native California www.heydaybooks.com/news
Spirit Magazine www.spiritmag.ca
Spirit of Aboriginal Youth Magazine www.saymag.com
Tribal College Journal www.tribalcollegejournal.org
Well Nations Magazine www.wellnations.com
Whispering Wind www.whisperingwind.com
Winds of Change www.wocmag.org